SpeedPro Series

TRACKDAY CAR PREPARATION

T0373710

VELOCE

DAVID HORNSEY

Choose the best upgrades for your trackday car • Tailored to your budget, your chosen car and what you want to get out of your trackdays
• Advice on the best modifications to deliver the results that you want

SPEEDPRO SERIES

978-1-901295-26-9

978-1-903706-72-5

978-1-845843-15-1

978-1-845840-05-1

978-1-845840-06-8

978-1-845840-19-8

978-1-845840-21-1

978-1-845840-23-5

978-1-845840-45-7

978-1-845840-73-0

978-1-845841-23-2

978-1-845841-42-3

978-1-845841-62-1

978-1-845841-86-7

978-1-845841-87-4

978-1-845842-07-9

978-1-845842-08-6

978-1-845842-62-8

978-1-845842-66-6

978-1-845842-89-5

978-1-845842-97-0

978-1-845843-55-7

978-1-845844-14-1

978-1-845844-33-2

978-1-874105-70-1

978-1-903706-17-6

978-1-903706-59-6

978-1-903706-68-8

978-1-903706-70-1

978-1-903706-75-6

978-1-903706-76-3

978-1-903706-77-0

978-1-903706-78-7

978-1-903706-80-0

978-1-903706-94-7

978-1-903706-99-2

978-1-904788-78-2

978-1-904788-84-3

978-1-904788-89-8

978-1-904788-91-1

978-1-904788-93-5

9781845842895

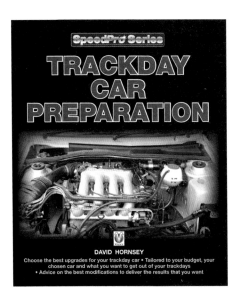

SpeedPro Series

TRACKDAY CAR PREPARATION

DAVID HORNSEY

Choose the best upgrades for your trackday car • Tailored to your budget, your chosen car and what you want to get out of your trackdays
• Advice on the best modifications to deliver the results that you want

www.veloce.co.uk

First published in May 2013 by Veloce Publishing Limited, Veloce House, Parkway Farm Business Park, Middle Farm Way, Poundbury, Dorchester, Dorset, DT1 3AR, England.
Fax 01305 250479/e-mail info@veloce.co.uk/web www.veloce.co.uk or www.velocebooks.com.

ISBN: 978-1-845844-83-7 UPC: 6-36847-04483-1

Contents

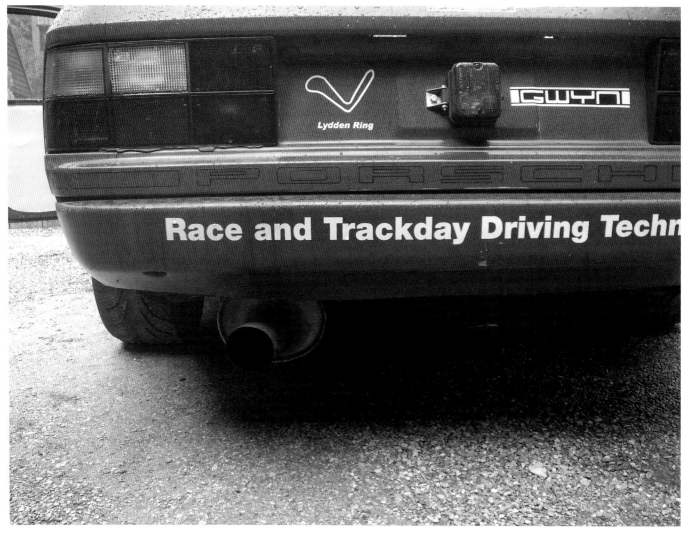

Lowered suspension, larger bore exhaust, sticky track tyres ... this car is ready for the track. (Author collection)

Introduction, Acknowledgements & Dedication

INTRODUCTION

I've always competed in motorsport on a budget, running my own cars (either by myself or with family and friends helping out), and I've learned the hard way many of the things you'll read here. I'm not a mechanical genius by any stretch of the imagination, and mechanical work is not something I've ever really got much in the way of enjoyment from (though, having said that, there's a great deal of satisfaction to be gained from driving

The author on track in a Porsche 924 built using much of the knowledge in this book. (Courtesy David Stallard)

The author's last 'work in progress,' earlier in its development. (Author collection)

something you've built yourself to the top step of the podium – especially when against far better funded and professionally-prepared outfits). As such, the cars I've been fortunate enough to race have mostly been 'works-in-progress,' with some parts more developed than others. So, writing this book was a chance to actually sit down and put all those snippets of knowledge together in a coherent form, and to research all those bits of 'gut-instinct' I'd gone along with over the years to find out if I was right and why it worked, whilst also sharing the knowledge of those experts who have helped me since I first got involved with cars.

Having gone through the process of preparing a car for track use several times over the years, and having seen others doing the same, my intention with the book was to give you some form of logical progression to making your own project; be it to go racing, to win a championship, or just to have a bit of fun. Your end goal will be unique, but this book will steer you in the right direction so you end up with a car that fulfils your ambitions. Best of luck, and keep it on the black stuff!

ACKNOWLEDGEMENTS

I'd like to thank everyone who has helped me understand anything mechanical over the years (or just sighed at my incompetence and done it for me). First and foremost, my late father Roy. Other than that, and in no particular order: Steve Miller, for learning along with me on recent projects, Tony Maryon of Whitchurch Motor Co (a very decent driver, by the way), Jamie Packham (also handy behind the wheel), the staff at J-Tech Automotive, the late Gwyn Jones, the guys at Lodge Sports for their advice, time and knowledge, and all the photographers who donated their work to this book.

DEDICATION

This book is dedicated to my sons, Ethan and Charlie, and to my wife, Rachel, for putting up with oil stains in the kitchen sink, and also to my late father, Roy, for doing all the mechanical stuff when I was younger so I didn't have to, and for all the moments of comedy gold (it still makes me smile when I think of hearing him say 'Ooops' whilst underneath the car ...).

Chapter 1
Getting started

Let's face it: driving on the roads these days is boring. With the increasing prevalence of speed cameras, 'traffic calming' measures, pot holes, and too many cars on the roads, the thought of 'going for a drive' is not as much fun as it used to be.

Back in the '70s and '80s you could take your Capri, Escort or Chevette out on a Sunday afternoon and have the back roads pretty much to yourself. With your lightweight (compared to today's cars), small-engined rockets, on skinny, high-profile tyres (bereft of much in the way of grip), everything would happen at a slower pace. Enthusiastic drivers could push their cars near, or even over their limits at relatively low speeds, fairly safe in the knowledge that there was unlikely to be anything coming the other way.

Fast forward 30-40 years, however, and the roads are a different place altogether. Cars are much more a necessary means of transport than an enjoyable experience, and yet, here we are in a golden age of performance cars. Never has there been such a wide choice of enthusiast-oriented cars available. The big guns in the motoring world are constantly releasing new super and 'hyper' cars which stretch the performance window beyond all recognition. Mainstream manufacturers are building driving-oriented special editions into their current lineups, or producing wholly new products purely for the spirited driver, and even humdrum saloons and hatchbacks are faster now than the sports cars of the '70s. But why? What's the point in it all if we can't enjoy them?

The answer is, of course, trackdays. Free from the officialdom and expense of going racing, trackdays are a fantastic opportunity to blow off some steam, explore the limits of your car, or develop your skills as a driver. In this book we'll delve into the world of trackdays, show you how you can get involved, and will be exploring everything from the basics of what type of event to take part in, right through to the type of cars to use, and how to modify them to make them better on track.

So, driving needn't be boring, not if you do it in the right place ...

TYPES OF TRACKDAYS
The term 'trackdays' covers a wide variety of events, so I think a brief overview of the opportunities available might be useful at this stage.

Experience days
Experience days encompass everything from flying in a balloon or paintballing, to mini spa breaks (spa as in mud baths and massages, not Spa as in Eau Rouge and 'Oh bollocks that's fast!'). For our purposes, the 'experiences' you get on these days are usually based at racing circuits or airfields, and use the local racing school to provide you with a few laps behind the wheel of the latest Ferrari or Aston Martin. Experience days are great for the casual car fan, and may well may be the only chance most people ever get to drive some of the world's exotica. However, for the enthusiast driver, they are not ideal. You don't get to drive alone, for example. An instructor will be with you throughout your few precious laps, but won't have time to assess your skills or build confidence in your ability to really let you push on. They'll be there primarily to keep the speed sensible, and you and the car (and them!) safe.

Mercedes and Porsche have both set up 'Experience Centres' in the UK, but they offer very different days out, and are targeted at very different markets. The Mercedes World centre at Brooklands in Surrey is very much a

A Ferrari on an Experience Day at Thruxton Race Circuit. (Courtesy Pieter van Beesten)

Porsche Experience Centre at Silverstone. (Courtesy Porsche GB)

Porsche on the 'Ice Hill' track at the Porsche Experience Centre. (Courtesy Porsche GB)

traditional experience day. The venue itself is a magnificent shrine to the past and present of Mercedes Benz, with some wonderful historic cars on display, plus the entire current model line, giving you the opportunity to buy one, new or secondhand, in the event your track experience impressed you enough. The driving itself is almost an afterthought. The small and fiddly track doesn't lend itself particularly well to executive barges lumbering around, and your time behind the wheel is fairly limited. It does make a great family day out, though, with off-road courses, rides (and drives) for the kids, and the wonderful Brooklands Museum next door.

The Porsche Experience Centre at Silverstone is a different prospect altogether. The venue is oriented much more towards the driver, and what he/she wants to get from the day. You'll usually spend half the day there, one-on-one with your instructor, driving on a variety of circuits, some with special low grip surfaces to practice car control.

You'll get more out of the day if you're a Porsche fan, but it's a great way to get some quality instruction in some great cars.

Manufacturer events

In the modern world there's no such thing as a bad car anymore. Gone are the days of brands being able to turn out turgid crap and expect the public to put up with it. Pretty much everything on the road today is a fairly good bit of kit. They all stay warm in winter, cool in summer, tune into whatever music you like, go, stop, corner, and carry shopping and passengers with decent aplomb. The thing is, in one regard, cars are generally SO good these days that no one gets to scratch the surface of their performance.

For example, let's compare a Ford Escort Mk2 RS2000 and the modern equivalent – a middle-of-the-range Ford Focus Mk3 1.6i Petrol. The Focus has more power, gets from 0-60 quicker, stops quicker, and can pull more lateral

G in the corners, yet has a smaller engine, is more economical, and has more creature comforts than you can shake a stick at. The thing is, as we've already seen, there's nowhere to exploit all this potential other than on a track. Manufacturers have cottoned on to this and many (including ones you wouldn't really think would be associated with track driving) now run events, especially on the launch of a new car or as part of a marketing push. Vauxhall is very good at the latter, running its VXR days across the UK each year to get people behind the wheel of its products. You'll tend to get a lot more track time on these types of days, compared to a traditional experience day, but they are less frequent, and to get onto 'launch' events you usually have to have shown some inclination to buy whatever is being launched for a dealer to invite you along.

It works, too. The number of cars sold off the back of these events is impressive, from Aston Martin right

Ferraris lined up ready to go on track on a trackday. (Courtesy Pieter van Beesten)

through to Citroën, the general public will be amazed at what a humble car can do in the right environment.

Corporate events

A well organised corporate event at the right venue can be a great day, even for a hardened track user. An event at Palmersports Bedford Autodrome (or Palm-ageddon as it's often referred to in the industry), gives you the chance to drive some proper race cars at proper speeds, with enthusiastic instructors pushing you on rather than being nannying ballast. The events last all day, and you get plenty of time in-car, and in a variety of cars and activities. Competition is often a major part of the day as well, enticing you to push on and drive the wheels off your car.

Handling days

On handling days, you're encouraged to push your car (usually the one you brought along with you, but some events supply cars), beyond its limits of grip, to allow you to practise the art of car control. These events vary wildly in terms of cost, venue, and experience; from the 'run-what-ya-brung' drift days at one end of the spectrum, right up to week-long ice driving holidays on replicas of F1 circuits carved into frozen lakes in Scandinavia. Other events along this line include the always popular Caterham Drift Days, where you spend the day doing figure-of-eights and 'donuts' around cones at the Surrey circuit, and the Academy Days run by Motorsport Events. Although usually a one- or two-at-a-time affair on track, to avoid the

risk of unwanted contact, the numbers taking part are often a lot lower than a traditional trackday, so you still get plenty of driving time.

Handling days are a great benefit, and mastering some of the skills will improve your track driving and general car control. Today's cars are so good, in terms of grip and chassis design, that when they do let go you're generally travelling very fast indeed. This has removed the learning process from the art of car control. These days, when the occasion arises where you need to use car control techniques, you're going so fast, and the situation arises so quickly, that you find you either have a natural talent for it or you are clambering out of a smoking wreck parked backwards in a hedge.

Learning the art of controlling oversteer on a handling day. (Courtesy Pieter van Beesten)

Airfield trackdays

Always my recommendation for your first track experience, airfield trackdays have lots of advantages over their circuit-based cousins. Firstly, they are cheaper. Airfields cost considerably less to hire than a circuit, so the trackday organiser has plenty of opportunity to bring the prices down, which is always a bonus. Secondly, there is nothing (or relatively little) to hit. Sooner or later when you're track driving you'll reach

Airfield days use cones to mark the circuit. (Courtesy Pieter van Beesten)

the point where you open your bag of 'talent' to find it is empty, and your fleeting feeling of being master of all you control turns into mild panic as you career off the track into the nearest available scenery. This will generally be a more frequent occurrence when you are new to track driving, and are building your skill levels and knowledge, hence my recommendation to start here first. Compared to circuits there are very few, or no, tyre walls, and no Armco, concrete barriers, gravel traps or trees, so when enthusiasm does outstrip ability, you've got plenty of space to slither gracefully

(as far as possible), to a stop before you compose yourself, snick it into first gear, and set off back to the pits to remove the seat cushion from between your butt cheeks. The best place to go for airfield trackdays is Motorsport Events. Whilst it didn't invent the idea it has been doing it a long time, and has a great range of venues, a good relationship with the MoD, which owns most of the airfields, and runs a very slick operation.

Circuit events

Let's be honest, this is probably what you're most interested in. The chance to

take your car out on the same hallowed tarmac that Lewis Hamilton and Jenson Button, Jason Plato and Matt Neal do battle on: circuits such as Silverstone, Brands Hatch and Donington Park. I can remember the first time I drove on circuits I'd only ever seen on TV; I got such a kick out of it. It's a really great experience, and tracks like Silverstone and Brands Hatch will give you corners and experiences that you won't find anywhere else in the world.

Depending on the venue, time of year, organiser, and popularity of the event, the day will either be run

Pushing on at a trackday. (Courtesy Pieter van Beesten)

A mix of track cars having fun. (Courtesy Jenny South)

in sessions (usually for Beginner/ Intermediate/Advanced groups), or will be Open Pit Lane (OPL). Depending on your level of experience and skill, there are advantages and disadvantages to both. Sessioned days mean you are only out on track with cars and drivers of a similar speed/skill level, so as a newbie you won't be constantly looking in your mirrors and worrying where the next hotshot in a GT3RS is coming from. Likewise, as an experienced track driver, you'll be held up less by novice drivers in the twisty bits. The downside is that it effectively cuts down your available track time. Though this does force you to take

time out, and gives you and your car a breather. An open pit lane event gives you the most freedom to go out when you want all day long, but what you find on track will be a complete cross-section of abilities, so you need to exercise a little bit of extra awareness and caution of the other drivers around you.

Circuit-based trackdays are either held by the circuit itself or a specialist trackday provider. The circuits which fall under the MSVR banner (Brands Hatch, Oulton Park, Snetterton, and Cadwell Park), all offer a variety of events, catering for everything from general trackdays to novice only events,

or marque specific days. Specialist trackday companies, such as Gold Track or Bookatrack, offer extensive trackday diaries at circuits all over the UK and Europe, and their professional organisations mean you get the best 'customer' experience you can hope for.

All the trackdays run by circuits and specialist organisers can be found on the excellent Trackday Diary on the MotorsportAds website: http://www. motorsportads.com/test-trackday-diary. htm

Nürburgring Nordschleife
The daddy of them all. The famous

The Nürburgring ... Mecca for trackday drivers. (Author collection)

(infamous?) North Loop is actually a public toll road, and has been since its completion in the 1920s. As such, any old Tom, Dick or Harry can turn up, pay the toll, and drive for a lap around the circuit. At over 14 miles (23 kilometres) long, the circuit is often quoted as having more corners in one lap than all the UK circuits put together. Whether it actually has or not I can't be bothered to count, but it's certainly a real challenge, and a great venue for the trackday enthusiast.

The area around the circuit in the Eifel region of Germany is a relatively poor area, with the circuit and its associated activities the main source of revenue. As such, the place is a motorsport and car-enthusiast Mecca, with every shop, restaurant, bar and hotel themed with motorsport memorabilia, and every major car manufacturer having a presence at the 'Ring, with research and development test centres.

The circuit itself is a mixture of mostly medium-speed corners with some very fast straights stretched over a rolling landscape, with minimal run-off, lots of expensive barriers to knock down, and more hills, blind crests and valleys than most mountain passes.

There has been a lot of political wrangling at the circuit over the last few years, with certain groups vying for control of the venue, and trying to force out some of the associated businesses. This upheaval has left a lot

The famous bar in the Dorint hotel at the Nürburgring, full of autographs and memorabilia; a perfect place to unwind after a day on track. (Author collection)

of uncertainty in the area and a bitter taste in the mouths of the local residents. The Industriefahrten or 'Industry Days,' occasions where manufacturers have free reign to use the circuit for test and development work, are on the increase, whilst Touristenfahrten, or 'Tourist Days,' are on the decrease, along with the opportunity for private trackday companies to hire the venue for events. Where this takes the circuit over the next few years is anyone's guess, but the current outlook isn't anywhere near as rosy as it should be. The track itself is pretty unique in its character (always be wary of a car that has been 'developed'

solely at the 'Ring, though, as it'll probably be a bit rubbish on any other circuit) and, apart from the sheer size, it can take a lifetime to become familiar with the venue, let alone master it.

Going to the 'Ring makes a great holiday for the car nut, but bear in mind the hidden costs. The laps themselves are reasonable value for money, though you will find it addictive and the 'just one more lap' mentality can quickly empty your wallet. Beware, though, that it is very expensive to make a mistake. If you go off, there's no run off to speak of; just a couple of metres of soggy, slick grass between the tarmac and the

Armco barrier. Whilst you'll be reeling at the cost of the damage to your car, the circuit itself kicks you when you're down by presenting you with an invoice for the damaged barriers, recovery, track closure costs, lost income from the track being closed, and anything else they can think of. It can turn a simple mistake into an expensive weekend. The 'Ring is always a track you build up to speed on, never go out pedal to the metal and 'see what happens.' Build up the pace only when you know the circuit and can assess the available grip.

Chapter 2
Basic driving techniques

This book isn't designed to be a bible on performance driving – there are other books out there which cover that subject very well, such as *Race and Trackday Driving Techniques,* also from Veloce. It does, however, cover the basics, so you've got a good grounding when you take your car out on track for the first time. In this chapter we'll cover the 'Ten Rules of Circuit Driving.'

THE TEN RULES OF CIRCUIT DRIVING

The following ten rules are the building blocks of trackday driving. Whenever you encounter a problem with a corner or a slow lap time, refer to these rules and, more often than not, you'll find one (or a combination) that will help you. Driving is an activity that is performed by the subconscious part of your brain. You don't

consciously think about pressing the pedals and turning the wheel; your subconscious performs these actions. Much like walking, you don't have to think 'left foot forward, right foot forward': you decide to walk down the street and your subconscious moves your legs and balances your body. Learning to drive on a circuit is, therefore, a process of teaching your subconscious a new

Going for it on a trackday. (Courtesy Pieter van Beesten)

Airfields give you lots of space to learn the basic skills of track driving. (Courtesy Pieter van Beesten)

Exotic cars can mix with trackday specials. (Courtesy Pieter van Beesten)

Torquing the wheel nuts. (Courtesy Pieter van Beesten)

was quite overwhelming. Now you're able to simply get into your car and drive it: your sub-conscious brain takes over the mechanics of driving, whilst you keep alert to what's going on around you and the route you're taking. In a similar way, the process of driving fast then becomes one of giving yourself and the car as little work to do as possible, leaving as much free mental capacity available to pick up the signals from the car so you know how close to the limits you are.

Rule 1: Seating and hand positions

This is an often overlooked but fundamental part of driving. A good 'connection' to the car is vital if you're to be able to control it and derive the maximum feedback from what it's doing.

When you learned to drive you would have been told to hold the wheel at the 'quarter to three' or 'ten to two' positions, and the same applies to circuit driving. Keeping both hands on the wheel is vital, as it keeps even pressure on both sides of the wheel and keeps it balanced. If the car hits a bump or a kerb, then you'll 'bounce' in the seat at a different rate to the car, and if you have just one hand on the wheel, it would be easy to transfer that bounce to the steering wheel, and inadvertently steer the car. If you have both hands on the wheel the steering effect of your 'bounce' is neutralised by having both hands moving the wheel in the same direction, therefore keeping the car's trajectory constant.

Keep your hands in this position as you steer the car, crossing your arms as you do so (like you were told never to do on your driving lessons!). By keeping your hands in the same place on the wheel, you'll always know where the front wheels are pointing, so you'll be able to react to a slide instantly without your brain having to think about where the straight-ahead position is. If you have to steer beyond the reach of your crossed arms, for example at a very tight hairpin, try to anticipate how far the wheel will go and use one hand to grab it in a different place before the turn to guide you round, or keep one hand in the original position on the wheel as a reference to the straight-ahead position. For a graphic illustration of the importance of this, think back to Nigel

set of skills, so it's important to learn them correctly. Your first few visits to a circuit will be mentally very challenging as you're confronted by these new skills. If you think back to when you first learned to drive a road car, you had to concentrate on accelerating, braking, steering, checking mirrors, using indicators, and watching out for other road users, all at the same time, which

Correct hand position. (Courtesy Pieter van Beesten)

Crossing the arms. (Courtesy Pieter van Beesten)

Mansell's ill-fated drive in a Mondeo Touring Car in 1993 at Donington. Whilst going through the Old Hairpin, the rear of the car broke away, and Nigel corrected by applying two turns of opposite lock. However, when the rear of the car stopped sliding he returned only one turn of lock, and the car speared off to the left. Mansell was heading to an accident even before he was collected by Tiff Needell who was following closely behind.

To achieve the correct seating position, you must be able to steer as previously described without over-stretching your arms. You should be able to sit normally in the seat, and, without stretching your shoulders forward, be able to comfortably place your wrists on top of the wheel (the top being the furthest point from you). This means that, when holding the wheel, you will

always have a small amount of flex in your elbows as you steer, regardless of where on the wheel your hands are. If your arms are locked straight as you steer, then you'll be using your shoulder muscles to control the direction of the wheel. Whilst these are very strong, they don't have a lot of subtlety, and the steering action will be jerkier. By having flex in your elbow, your forearm muscles will have a more precise and subtle control of the wheel. To obtain this seating position you may have to have the back of your seat in a more vertical position to that which you are used to on the road. This gives you a better feel for the stability and balance of the car as you drive.

There are, perhaps, three or four corners in the country where you might need to release the wheel: the final hairpin on the Croft circuit, Hatchets

hairpin at Pembrey, the Mountain cut through on the Park circuit at Cadwell Park, and the Shaws hairpin at Mallory Park. Other than at these locations, you should never need to release your hands from the wheel other than to change gear.

The position of your feet is also very important, especially as you learn to heel-and-toe shift. You'll spend more of the lap on the throttle than on the brakes, so the heel of your right foot should be positioned directly below the accelerator pedal. When you brake, your heel should stay in the same relative location, but your toes should move left to meet the brake pedal. This is also important when you come to left foot braking, because if the heel of your right foot is under the brake pedal when you're accelerating, it may get in the way of your left foot as it comes across to operate the brake. At

Correct seating position. (Courtesy Pieter van Beesten)

The grey line shows the consequences of turning in too early. (Author collection)

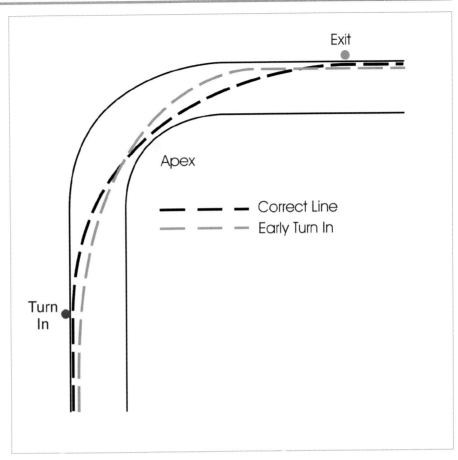

Rule 2: Vision

Where you look when driving is very important, as we tend to follow our line of sight. Don't concentrate on the road just in front of the car – this will give very little time for planning and preparing for the approaching corners. Instead, always try to look as far ahead on the road as possible, and, as you exit one corner, look to the turn-in point for the next bend. As you approach the braking area, look at the apex of the corner and you'll be better able to judge your braking. After initiating your braking, look to the turn-in point and, just before reaching it, look back to the apex again to see where you're going. At the apex, look through to the exit point and repeat the cycle again.

By looking down the road at the next bend as you leave the preceding one, you will have formed a mental picture of the corner before you arrive at it, allowing you to drive the corner more on autopilot, and giving you spare mental capacity to react to the vehicle.

Rule 3: Line

Use the cones on the track to guide your line. The turn-in will always feel later than your instinct demands, but trust it is correct. Look at the accompanying diagram and you can see that the earlier you turn-in to a corner the tighter the apex becomes, resulting in a need to adjust your speed and line mid-bend. If you turn-in at the correct place, the whole corner should become a constant, or opening, radius. Through the turn try to use the full width of the track to minimise the amount of turn required, and keep the car going in as straight a line as possible. The straighter the car is travelling, the less difference there is between the trajectory of the front and rear wheels, so the less resistance there is between them, and the faster the car can travel. Also, the tighter you turn the slower you must go, so try to turn as little as possible.

Most people hold a common misconception about what a corner is: that is, the part of the track where the tarmac is changing direction through a radius, marked by a painted kerb on the inside edge (the area around the yellow marker in the accompanying diagram). From a driving point of view, however, this is incorrect. The corner is the point, back on the preceding straight, where you turn the wheel into the bend. Again, looking at the diagram, it's by the red 'Turn-In' cone. The fact that you get close to, or run over, the kerb on the inside by the 'Apex' cone is merely a confirmation that you got the corner right. All your inputs regarding your trajectory around the corner are decided at the moment you turn the wheel.

When you turn into the bend from the turn-in cone, do not head directly for the apex cone. Instead, describe an arc

these speeds, you don't want to get your feet tangled!

Trackday action. (Courtesy Pieter van Beesten)

so that when you reach the apex you are able to continue on the same radius all the way to the exit of the corner.

Avoid adjusting the steering in the bend. Once you've turned-in, keep the steering lock constant and you will, if you have turned-in and apexed at the correct positions, successfully complete the corner. Adding lock mid-bend will always result in a slower lap time, and usually a spin. Imagine that you've turned-in to the corner right on the ragged edge of adhesion, you are travelling as fast as you can around the radius of the turn; any faster and you'll lose grip and slide wide. Imagine, then, at the apex you suddenly add extra steering, tightening the line without the car reducing speed. The car will instantly spin-off, as you're asking it to

turn tighter than it's capable of doing at the speed it's going.

Rule 4: Braking

Braking must always be carried out in a straight line. This keeps the vehicle stable and reduces the risk of spinning-out. Due to the way physics determines that bodies move through the atmosphere, cars are only really happy when travelling in a straight line; they don't particularly like heavy braking, and they definitely don't like going around corners. When you're slowing the car under braking, the momentum of the vehicle dictates that it wishes to carry on at the same speed on the same straight trajectory it was on before you braked. Because the body of the car is trying to carry on, but the wheels are trying to

slow its progress, the chassis will pull forward. The only point of flexibility in the equation is the suspension, so, as the chassis tries to continue forward, its weight will become more concentrated on the front wheels and rise up off the rear wheels. This increase in weight on the front tyres and decrease in weight on the rear tyres will affect the level of grip the tyres are able to provide. Tyres will grip the road surface because their weight, and any weight supported by them, pushes them into the road surface, causing friction. Therefore, the greater the weight on a tyre the more grip it will provide.

Under braking, the front tyres will have more grip than the rear tyres. If you look at the diagrams in 'Rule 6: Smoothness, weight distribution and the scale of ten,' you will see how braking shifts the weight over the front tyres. If you try to change direction under braking, the front of the car will, more than likely, accept the change in direction due to the increased grip the front tyres are experiencing. However, the rear tyres have a dramatically reduced level of grip, so they will be less likely to be able to accept the direction change, and, as the rear of the car will still be 'wanting' to travel in a straight line, the car will begin to spin inwards. This effect will be dramatically increased with cars with a rearward weight bias, such as the Porsche 911 and Lotus Elise, as they'll have greater momentum at the rear trying to travel in a straight line.

The other thing to consider about braking is to do it smoothly. If you suddenly stomp on the brake, then the front tyres are either neutrally-loaded or, if you were previously accelerating,

lightly-loaded, so they'll offer little grip, will cause the front brakes to lock, and will reduce your stopping and steering abilities. On cars fitted with ABS (Anti-locking Braking System), stomping on the pedal will engage the ABS, again reducing your stopping ability as the brakes will pulse (only being engaged for part of the time). When you initially apply the brake it must be relatively gently, then build up the brake pressure to the required amount for the corner. The initial gentle deceleration will redistribute some of the weight of the chassis onto the front wheels giving them more grip, then, as the brake pressure increases, the weight over the front wheels, and hence their grip, will also increase, leading to very efficient braking.

Similarly, when you complete the braking, release the pedal gently. If you suddenly jump off the pedal, the compressed front springs will rebound

and extend beyond their neutral point, and the front tyres will have a reduced load on them and, therefore, reduced grip. This will result in the front wheels sliding as you enter the corner (understeer). By releasing the pedal smoothly, the front springs will be controlled in their rebound by the reducing brake pressure, thereby only returning to a neutral position and maintaining grip on the front wheels.

A good descriptive term for applying and releasing the brake correctly is to 'roll on' and 'roll off' the brake pedal.

Rule 5: Accelerating

The speed at which you turn-in to the corner should remain constant from the turn-in point to the apex. At the apex, or clipping point of the corner, you should be able to see the exit, and, if you've turned-in at the right place

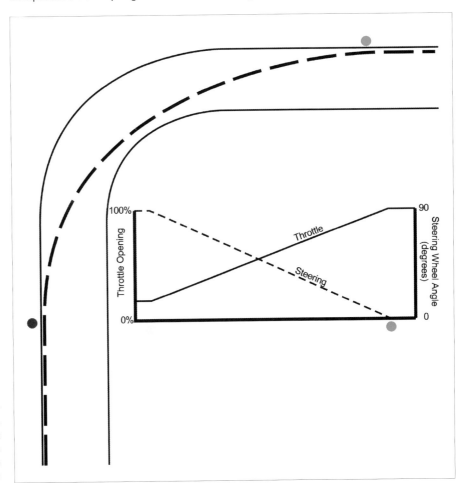

As you can see from the diagram, as you pass the apex (yellow marker) gradually increase the throttle as you unwind the steering lock so that as you pass the exit (green marker) you are straight on the wheel (0 degrees) and flat (100%) on the throttle. (Author collection)

and apexed at the right place, you'll be able to see you're on the correct line to the exit point. Then, and only then, at the apex, do you start to accelerate. As with the other controls on the car, do this smoothly, if you stomp on the throttle you'll suddenly be requesting a lot of forward traction from tyres that are at or near their limit of sideways traction. You'll easily overcome the ultimate traction available (check out the 'scale of ten' in the next rule), and the driven wheels will spin causing a sudden understeer (front-wheel drive), or oversteer (rear-wheel drive). So, from the apex to the exit you should progressively open the throttle so that by the time you're at the exit of the corner you're flat on the power. As you open the throttle, you should also gently unwind the steering lock so that you're straight at the exit. As the need for traction, or forward grip, from the tyre increases, the demand for sideways grip must decrease to avoid overcoming the overall grip potential of the tyre.

Rule 6: Smoothness, weight distribution, and the 'scale of ten'

When driving quickly, it's important to operate all the car's controls smoothly. Steer smoothly and gently, without sudden movements. Brake and accelerate by 'squeezing' the pedals, not stomping on them, and release them gently. Not being smooth causes the vehicle to become unbalanced, leading to a loss of traction and a spin. You're sitting in a ton and a half of metal whose trajectory is determined by four small contact patches of rubber, so you need to move that weight around gently to keep the tyres gripping.

Imagine you're trying to move a heavy box across the floor: if you kick it, it will move quite freely as it has received a sudden shock. However, if you lean on it, and gently build up the pressure until it moves, you'll need a lot of strength to break the friction with the floor. The same principle applies to your car: be gentle with it and the grip will reward you; be aggressive with it, and the easier it will break traction and get out of shape. Also, be aware that the faster you're travelling the more energy will be involved in every input you make. Think of the speed of steering input that you will perform when parking in the supermarket carpark compared to the amount of steering you will use on a motorway. The faster you go the smoother you must be.

As you can see from the accompanying diagrams, as you brake, accelerate, and corner, the weight applied to each tyre alters. The grip potential of the tyre, its friction with the road surface, is affected by this weight: the more weight applied to the tyre the more it is pushed into the surface of the tarmac, and the greater the friction (and, therefore, grip). Using the brakes, throttle and steering will alter the grip balance of your car around the circuit, and operating the controls smoothly makes it easier to control transitions between these different characteristics. Also, it's important to minimise your input to the car. Each adjustment you make, be it accelerating, braking or steering, will move the weight of the vehicle around as shown, and, as the weigh is added and removed, you'll be changing the grip available to the tyre.

The 'scale of ten'											
Total grip available:	10	10	10	10	10	10	10	10	10	10	10
Longitudinal or traction grip used:	0	1	2	3	4	5	6	7	8	9	10
Lateral or turning grip available:	10	9	8	7	6	5	4	3	2	1	0

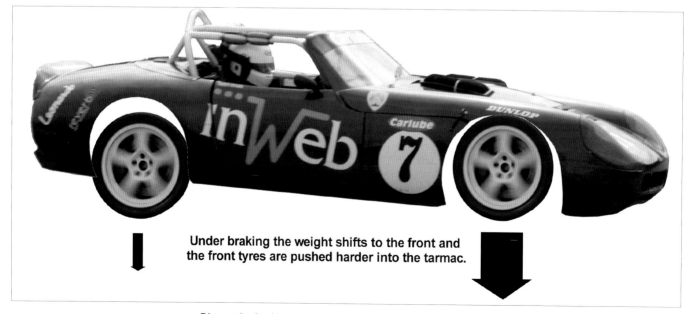

Under braking the weight shifts to the front and the front tyres are pushed harder into the tarmac.

Dive under braking. (Courtesy David Hornsey/Steve Clarke)

Under acceleration the weight shifts to the rear and the rear tyres are pushed harder into the tarmac.

Squat under acceleration. (Courtesy David Hornsey/Steve Clarke)

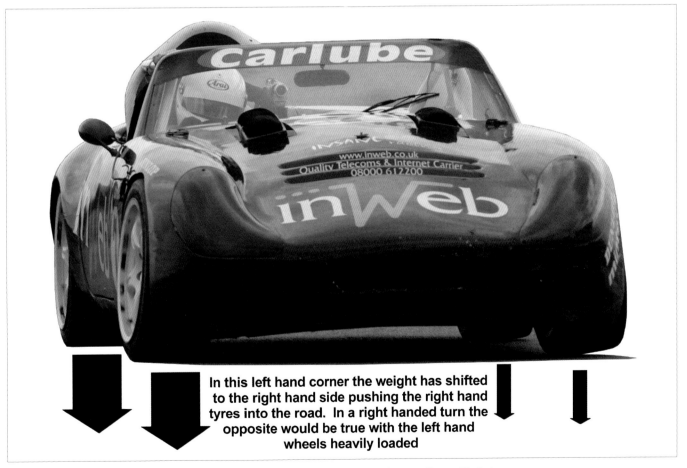

In this left hand corner the weight has shifted to the right hand side pushing the right hand tyres into the road. In a right handed turn the opposite would be true with the left hand wheels heavily loaded

Roll when cornering. (Courtesy David Hornsey/Steve Clarke)

Therefore, if you're constantly playing with the steering angle or coming on and off the power in the middle of a bend, you'll constantly shift weight distribution and grip levels. This will make the car more difficult to control, and you won't be able to corner at the limit of the car's ability.

Furthermore, the constant adjustments you'll need to make to compensate for all these extra inputs require additional mental capacity. By minimising your inputs to one brake per corner, one turn per corner, and one acceleration per corner, the car will have less to deal with, and you'll have less to concentrate on, allowing you and your car to perform to your utmost abilities.

When accelerating, braking and turning, always bear in mind the amount of grip available at each tyre, and how it's being used. As the previous diagrams show, as more weight is applied to a tyre, the more grip it will have. However, there will always be a limit to the grip available, and you must balance the longitudinal and lateral grip requests so as not to exceed this limit. Let's say this total amount of grip available is 'ten points' of grip. The actual frictional force will vary, as mentioned above, but we will use this simplified 'ten points' system. If a tyre has only one job to do, ie cornering or braking, it can do that job to its maximum ability, using all ten points. If you then decide to do two jobs with that tyre, ie cornering AND braking, it can't do either as effectively, as it needs to use, say, five of its points to brake and five to go round the corner. Therefore, to get the best performance out of the tyre only do one thing at a time.

Rule 7: Down-shifting
This can be split into two topics: 'Where' and 'How.'

Where
When approaching a corner, take note of the correct gear required for the bend before you begin braking. Then, simply split the braking zone into equal portions, and change gear at each transition between portions. For example, if you're in fifth gear and the approaching corner is a third gear bend, change from fifth to fourth one third of the way through the braking

zone, and then change from fourth to third two thirds of the way through the braking zone. If you only need to change down one gear, do it half way through the braking zone. This ensures that you don't over-rev the engine by downshifting at too high a speed, and that you've completed all your gear movements and re-engaged the clutch before you reach the turn-in point for the corner.

How
Down-shifting is a sure-fire way of unbalancing the vehicle, so you must shift as smoothly as possible to minimise this effect. Firstly, it's important to keep your foot on the brake when changing gear. This sounds like common sense, but a lot of drivers with only road experience will release the brake as they depress the clutch, and only reapply the brake once the next gear has been selected and the clutch engaged. Releasing the brake, particularly when the clutch is disengaged, means the car will run away with itself, with nothing slowing it down. Also, if you think of the time spent off the brake whilst changing gear, you could move that period to the beginning of the braking zone to initiate the braking later thereby reducing your lap time.

Move the gearlever across the gate briskly, but without forcing it or rushing the change, as this can lead to mistakes, missed gears, 'buzzed engines,' or, again, an unbalancing of the car. As you release the clutch, come up slowly, as the engine revs will be in the process of dropping from the previous gear, but will have to accelerate up the majority of the rev range as the clutch re-engages. If you release the clutch too quickly, the engine will not be able to increase its revs in time, and will slow the drivetrain, effectively locking the driven wheels. This is less likely to happen in a front- or four-wheel drive vehicle, though, as the driven wheels have a lot of weight and grip due to the brakes being on and the front of the car being loaded up. In a rear-wheel drive car, however, this situation is especially prevalent, and you must be extra smooth on the clutch to avoid the sensation of the handbrake being applied mid-braking.

Rule 8: Slow in, fast out
This is the mantra of performance driving. Your lap time around a circuit is not determined by how fast you enter a corner but by how fast you exit the bend. Look at the three accompanying diagrams. Diagram one shows the fastest turn-in apex and exit speeds we could drive through a corner if we took a constant radius, which, as you can see, is 60mph (97kph) on turn-in, 60mph (97kph) on apex, and 60mph (97kph) on exit. Diagram two shows the same corner but a 5mph (8kph) higher turn-in speed. As you can see, to be able to turn-in quicker you must turn-in slightly earlier to have a shallower entry radius. However, this radius cannot be sustained throughout the corner without running off the track, so the radius must be gradually tightened and, to avoid losing control of the car as the radius tightens, the speed must reduce. So a 65mph (105kph) turn-in leads to a 60mph (97kph) apex and 55mph (89kph) exit, the same average speed through the corner but faster between the turn-in and apex. Diagram three turns this around. By turning-in at 55mph (89kph) we can turn in later and a bit tighter, getting more of the corner out of the way early on. We can then increase our speed to 60mph (97kph) by the apex and continue to increase to 65mph (105kph) on the exit. Again, we have an average of 60mph (97kph) through the corner, but we've lost time on the way into the bend. Importantly, though, we are 10mph (16kph) quicker on the exit than the car in diagram two, which means we are 10mph (16kph) quicker onto the following straight, which is an advantage that will pay us back all the way up the straight.

Turning-in quicker means you'll only be quicker from the turn-in point to the apex of the bend. However, exiting quicker means you'll be quicker from the apex, past the exit, and all the way down the next straight to the next braking point; a much greater distance.

Rule 9: Spinning
Sooner or later your enthusiasm will get the better of your talent, and you will spin. When you've asked too much of your car and tyres, don't panic. Once the car has reached the point where it cannot be saved from a spin, simply

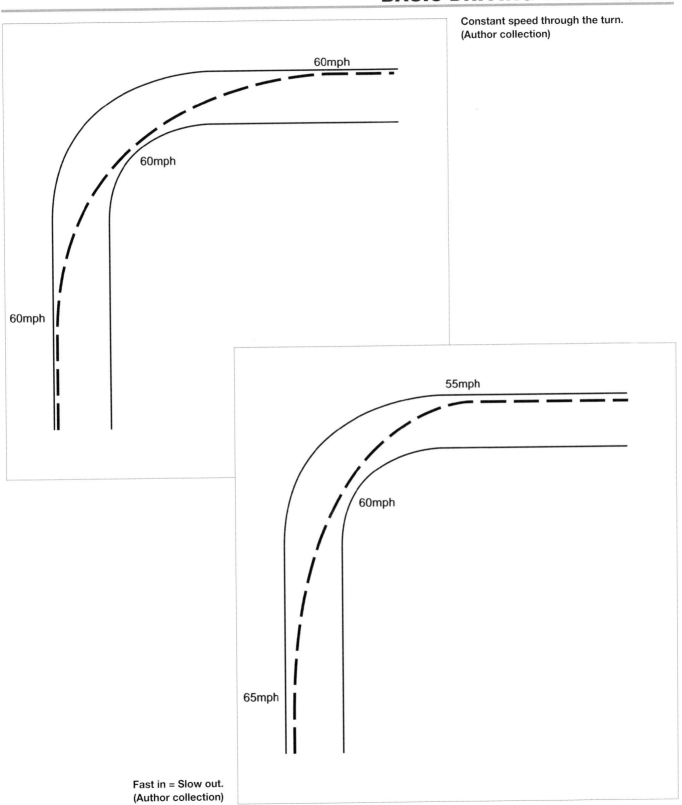

Constant speed through the turn.
(Author collection)

60mph

60mph

60mph

55mph

60mph

65mph

Fast in = Slow out.
(Author collection)

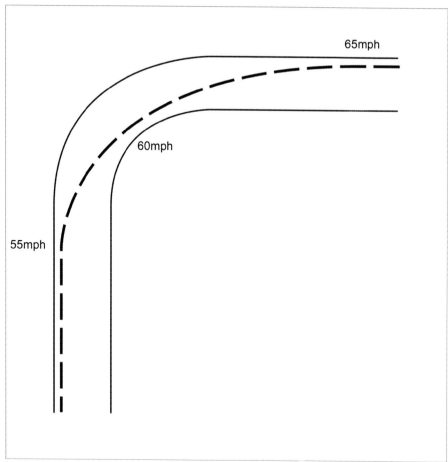

apply the brakes hard and dip the clutch. Applying the brakes will stop the car from rolling back into traffic or a barrier, and will bring the car to a rest as quickly and as safely as possible. Dipping the clutch will keep the engine running.

If you haven't managed to get the clutch down in time, and the engine has stalled, it may struggle to re-fire. If the driven wheels rotated backwards at any time the engine would have turned backwards, reversing the ignition sequence in each cylinder. This will mean that a few turns of the engine will be required on the starter motor to clear the cylinders to allow the engine to fire again.

You'll need to get the clutch down earlier than you think. Once the car is 90 degrees to the direction of travel, the driven wheels will no longer be turning (they'll be sliding sideways across the

tarmac), so, although the car is still moving at a potentially rapid pace, the engine will have stopped.

Rule 10: Taking instruction

This is the fastest way to learn a track and improve your driving when on a trackday. An experienced, professional instructor sat alongside you can bring massive speed gains in a short amount of time, but you have to work with him/her to get the best out of the experience. There's no point trying to impress your instructor by attempting to show you're the next Lewis Hamilton. He/she will have sat next to hundreds of drivers, and will have seen all levels of ability. Your instructor wants to know by the time you have reached the first corner that he/she can trust you to do what's asked. He/she will have two objectives when in your car: firstly, that you show a degree of progression, and; secondly,

that he/she stays alive long enough to get paid! As you arrive at the first corner the instructor will ask you to brake. Do so immediately, smoothly, and positively, even if you think you'll be going way too slow for the bend. Listen intently to the instructions on where to place the car and how to accelerate out of the bend, and follow them precisely. This will dramatically increase your instructor's confidence in you, and he/she will start to push you to go faster, knowing that you'll listen to, and follow, every instruction.

If you career into that first bend with minimal braking, and nowhere near the cone you were asked to get close to, the instructor will know he/she will have to spend the whole time with you trying to get you to slow down and listen; which, ultimately, is a waste of time for you and a stressful half hour for the instructor.

The author instructing at Thruxton in Hampshire. (Courtesy Pieter van Beesten)

The instructor is trying to help you, so help them by listening and acting on their instructions.

Remember, the instruction process is two-way. If you have any questions or don't understand the importance or relevance of an instruction, ask. Instructors are, by and large, a friendly bunch, and want to see you progress (it satisfies their egos to see their pupils improving).

A lot can be learned even when not driving, and the instructor is able to explain, in detail, what is the best approach.
(Courtesy Pieter van Beesten)

Chapter 3

Types of cars to use on a trackday

There are a number of choices to make when you decide to take the plunge into trackday driving. If it's your first ever event, you might be wise to take your everyday road car. This gives you the opportunity to try the trackday world and see if it appeals to you. It will also let you see what else is out there, and make a more informed decision about what you want to do with your trackday car of choice in the long-term.

You can, of course, continue to use your everyday road car; modern cars are getting better and better track manners, especially if the car is a sporty version to begin with. The tyre and suspension combination will make the car fairly stable on the track. Be warned, though, that your regular insurance probably won't cover you on track, and if your car is a lease or hire car you'll more than likely be barred from taking part in track events as part of the contract. It might be worth investing in a set of track wheels and tyres as well. You don't want to be backing off all day on track to avoid putting your tyres through too much wear so you can get home legally and safely.

There's a very good argument for having a second, track only, car.

Secondhand cars are relatively cheap these days, and taking this option reduces the risk to your day-to-day transport. Incidents on trackdays are rare, but you're going to the circuit to push yourself and your car to the limits, so, sooner or later, you'll be involved in some sort of incident. The vast majority of the time the worst outcome is a quick spin, a visit to a gravel trap, or a ticking off from the trackday organiser. However, on rare occasions you will make contact with something solid. If your car does get damaged, and it's the same car you were going to use to get home in/go to work in the next day, then you're in a bit of a pickle. A dedicated track car has just one purpose: fun. It doesn't need any compromises, such as being able to get your luggage in the boot for your holiday, or return really good fuel economy, or have really compliant suspension to cope with potholes. A dedicated track car is whatever you want it to be: a stripped-out hot-hatch; a bare-bones Lotus 7-alike; a big-engined muscle car; front-wheel drive; rear-wheel drive; four-wheel drive; a particular marque, etc. We'll be looking into preparing a trackday car from a road car later in the book, but the starting point will primarily

be defined by the main issue in anything involving cars and motorsport-type activities ... money. How much can you budget for your car, and what are your plans to improve its track manners?

Getting a track car raises a couple of issues straight away. Do you keep it road legal, for example, and drive it to and from the circuit? Or, do you invest in a trailer and tow vehicle and keep it as a track-only car? Whilst the latter option gives you greater flexibility for tuning and developing your car into a track specific car, it does mean there's the extra investment in the tow vehicles, along with the need for somewhere to store them if you decide to buy rather than rent. This investment might outweigh, or be outweighed by, the cost of road tax and road insurance for your track toy if you decide to drive it to and from the track, and also limits some of your tuning options if you need to keep it road legal. For example, you won't be able to put an air intake where the headlight should be, you'll need that headlight to get home, and you probably won't want to make some modifications, as it will become too compromised as a road car. The other issue is one we touched on earlier. If you were to experience an accident or

Almost anything can go on track, even the most unlikely of cars! (Author collection)

BMW E36 325: a great track car made even better with a few tweaks. (Author collection)

a component failure you might be stuck if the track car was also due to be your ride home. Only you can deal with these considerations and decisions, and they depend on your budget, expectations and circumstances. There's no right or wrong answer.

Let's look at a range of budgets, and get a rough idea about what's available.

At the very bottom end of the scale many people buy a track car from the bargain section of the local classifieds, with the intention of running it till it breaks, then buy another one. If your main focus is cheap fun and/or driving development, this is probably the cheapest way to go about it. You don't need to worry much about maintenance, apart from checking it has oil and water; that the wheels are securely tightened, and that the brakes work. If anything major fails or falls off, your local scrapyard will collect it whilst you go and get your next track weapon. In this way,

over the course of a couple of seasons you might also get the opportunity to drive lots of different types of car to expand your track driving skills.

Moving up the scale, for two to three thousand pounds you can pick up some fantastic cars from the '80s and '90s. They'll make great track cars, and are generally easy to work on (with less electronic trickery in them than modern cars), allowing the home mechanic more options in tuning and upgrading. Parts are often cheap, and upgrade parts are plentiful as well, so these make great beginner trackday cars that you can develop over time into extremely quick and competent track tools. The selection of cars in this price bracket is huge, with anything from Porsche 944s to Clio 16vs, Golf GTis to BMW E36 M3s, early Subaru Imprezzas to Audi S3s, Focus STs to MX5s, and Seat Cupras to Nissan 200SXs. This list is almost endless and you can really find almost anything to your taste.

Once you get into the £5k+ bracket, you'll be looking at some fairly modern hot hatches, like Astras and Corsa VXRs, Megane R26s and 225s, early Golf R32s or later GTis, BMW's Mini Cooper S, or even an early E46 M3, and, if you really want to start an adventure on and off the track, you can pick up TVR Chimeras for that sort of money. Again, the choice here is huge, and, by the time your budget stretches to £10k, you'll be looking at some properly good bits of kit, including 996 Porsche Carreras, BMW Z4s, Mitsubishi Evos, Lotus Elises, modern hot hatches, etc.

The cars I've mentioned here are all at the bottom end of their respective price brackets, but it really does show what fantastic cars are available for relatively little money these days. Being cars at the bottom of their price bracket they will tend to be higher mileage or less well looked after examples, but it doesn't really matter if the car is a little scruffy if you're only using it for a few

Mazda 3 MPS, wolf in sheep's clothing and a low-cost, everyday track weapon. (Courtesy Pieter van Beesten)

Radical – the purpose-built track car. (Courtesy Jenny South)

trackdays a year. As for the mechanicals, make sure there are no obvious signs of impending failure when you look at the car (such as excessive smoke from the exhaust, difficult to engage gears, noisy engines, knocking suspension, etc). If you have a particular car in mind, do some research on internet forums and via owners clubs to see what common issues you should look out for beforehand. Modern cars are so well designed that the mechanicals really can do astronomical miles if looked after, so don't be too put off by a car with a hundred thousand miles on the engine, if the car has been regularly and competently serviced it will still keep going for plenty of miles yet. Plus, on older cars, replacement engines and gearboxes are also relatively cheap, as the cars are so cheap in the first place, so major failure won't necessarily break the bank.

Beyond the price points discussed above, you'll be delving into much more modern machinery. Until recently, the trend has been for each new model of car to be bigger and heavier than the preceding one, and to be filled with more toys and electronic frippery. Whilst this is fine for a road car, weight is the enemy of track driving, and the extra electronic monitoring and assistance to the mechanicals adds an additional complexity to the maintenance of the car.

If you have the skills and the tools to keep the more modern cars up to scratch, then these can be some very rewarding cars, but, if you don't, they can become very expensive.

Beyond £20k you start to come across a relatively new phenomenon: a trackday car built by a small or even mainstream manufacturer to tap into the trackday market. Big players have released trackday editions of their already pumped-up hot hatches, such as Vauxhall with its Corsa and Astra VXR Nürburgring Editions, as lighter, more powerful, stiffer and grippier versions. At the other end of the spectrum, manufacturers such as Radical have sprung up, and created a very successful niche for themselves in (only just) road legal, track sports cars, which rely on light weight and aerodynamics to give massively fast cornering speeds. In this bracket you should also see the ubiquitous Caterham/Westfield-type cars; a design that has stood the test of time extremely well. The Seven is a truly remarkable car, and, in its many guises, offers different experiences to different drivers. The smaller-engined cars are often on narrower tyres, and are all about conserving momentum and carrying speed through the corners, whereas the larger-engined cars are more about throttle control, setting up the car in the corner to use the torque and power to fire you down the next straight. The derivatives powered by motorbike engines offer a high-rev, high-intensity, knife-edge driving experience.

Developing any of these cars away from their roadgoing origins towards being purpose-built track tools is an exciting and rewarding experience, but always try to balance it with what you are using the car for. If the car is still going

to be a form of daily or even occasional transport, then going too extreme on the development can lead to a very awkward and difficult car to drive out on the road. Conversely, leaving it too original will eventually become frustrating on the track as you come up against dynamic inadequacies. Furthermore, it may also be potentially more expensive, as the extra weight you're carrying around with all those road-car niceties will wear out brakes, tyres, bushes, bearings, clutches, etc, that bit quicker.

At this price point you're also getting into the realms of ex-race cars. These can be bought for any amount of money, from a race-ready £300 eBay find to a £400,000 GT3 car, but those in the former group are generally more trouble than they're worth, and the latter are, I suspect, out of your budget. From £10k upwards you can get some really nice privately- or manufacturer-built race cars – good, reliable and fast track tools, with all the hard work already done. One extra thing to bear in mind if you go down this route, though, is that your budget for your track car also needs to include a trailer and tow vehicle. If you're planning on only doing a couple of events a year, you may find it cheaper to rent a van and trailer each time you go out; it saves on insurance, tax and storage costs, but isn't necessarily as flexible as having your own kit. Also, bear in mind that a race car will end up being more expensive to maintain than a road car, as the components for it are generally more specialised and more expensive. It's a running joke that out of two identical alloy wheels, the one painted white and called the 'Motorsport' wheel will be twice the price!

Again, if you have the budget, skills, and tools to run one, then these will make a great trackday car. The car will be built to a specific set of regulations, but there's nothing stopping you from altering or improving it yourself, though this will probably be quite expensive as the car will have a lot of good kit on it already. If you do alter the car, it's always worth keeping the components you take off (so if you ever decide to sell it on, you can include the bits to make it eligible for the series or championship it originally came from).

If we start to talk about BIG money, we'll see some extra special cars from

manufacturers who are really pushing the boundaries of modern supercars. These are real halo cars, or dream machines, posters of which would easily take pride of place on the bedroom walls of many a teenager. Cars like the Porsche 911 GT3RS, Ferrari Scuderias, Aston Martin V12 Vantage and V8 Vantage S, Lamborghini's Superleggeras, AMG Black Editions, Noble M600, to name but a few. There are those out there with the funds and the desire to modify these cars as well, but as they stand they are all fantastic trackday cars that will, for the most part, be happy with the daily commute. As with all modern cars, though, maintaining these over track events will be more expensive than older cars, but the cars are so well engineered that they are generally a turnkey experience. As long as they have oil and water in them, and the tyres are inflated, you can abuse them all day on track and, at the end of the day, they will drive home like they have never set wheel on a track.

It's also worth touching on a sensitive issue now, which is only going to become worse as time goes by: noise. We live in a country where, apparently, the needs of the many are far less important than the opinion of the individual (it's funny, I was always told at school that we lived in a democracy), and there seems to be a tendency for people to move next door to something noisy like a race track, airport or motorway, and then complain about the noise. Hence, circuit owners are having to abide by ever-stricter noise requirements. What this means for you is that the trackday you're going to will almost certainly have a noise restriction. This is usually in the form of a static noise test performed before your car goes out on circuit, and you'll need to rev your car to approximately three-quarters of its maximum rev range whilst an environmental scrutineer measures the level of noise half a metre from the exhaust, at a 45-degree angle from the outlet.

The actual noise level permitted will vary from venue to venue, and even day to day at some tracks, as there'll be a set number of 'noisy' and 'quiet' days it's allowed to run. There are even tracks where, on certain days, you're not allowed to make tyre noise (which

Porsche GT3: track car for the road? (Courtesy Jenny South)

Intense concentration obvious as this McLaren 'hyper' car is guided through the wet. (Courtesy Jenny South)

kind of defeats the object of going on a trackday if you can't push your car to its limits). Increasingly, circuits are also being required to monitor drive-by noise levels at various points around the site. It's much harder to know if your car will pass or not, though, as the speed and load of the engine, exhaust direction, distance to the microphone, speed of travel, surrounding vehicles, buildings and barriers, even the weather on the day, will all have their part to play in the noise received by the monitoring microphone.

The planning permits the circuits hold with their local authorities will be so sensitive on the issue of noise that there's more than likely no chance to argue your case or 'slip through the net.' If your car is exceeding the noise limit, you'll be sent home. If you think your car may be too noisy for a particular day, see if you can find someone with a noise meter to test it before you go, or try to compare it with a car you know passes the tests. Ex-race cars and motorcycle-engined and other high-revving cars are often very close to, or over, the limits, so take extra precautions if you fall into one of those brackets. If you do need to make your car quieter, it's always best to go down the permanent or semi-permanent route, ie welding or bolting on additional permanent or temporary silencers to your exhaust, rather than the temporary measure of stuffing loads

Aston Martin GT4 makes a great turnkey trackday toy. (Courtesy Jenny South)

of wadding up the exhaust to muffle the sound, as this will blow out after a few laps, and you'll risk failing the drive-by noise limit.

This situation will only get more difficult, so we must all work together to keep our cars relatively quiet to avoid making life more difficult for everyone.

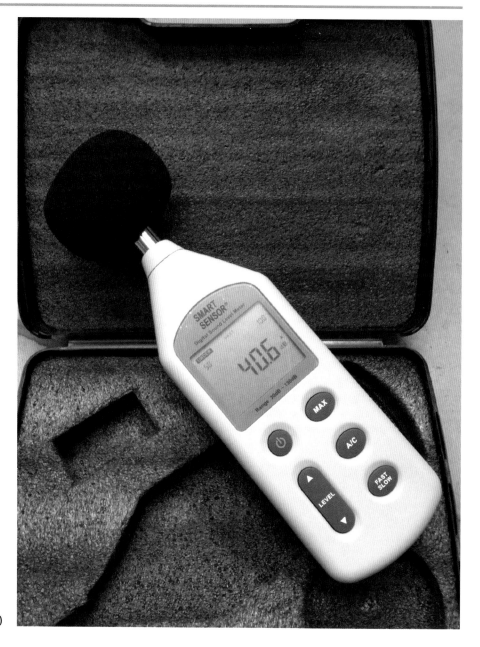

Noise meter. (Author collection)

Chapter 4
Cost-effective upgrades

When you start modifying your car for track work, there's a lot you can do to improve on its humble road car origins. The sky's the limit, really; though what you can achieve will depend on your budget. An often-asked question in motorsport is: "How much will it cost?" To which the truthful answer is: "How fast do you want to go?"

The good thing about trackday cars compared to race cars is that you're building them to be fun rather than for outright pace, so you need develop it only as much as you want, and only in the direction you want. Faster isn't always better. If you look at the recently released Toyota/Subaru coupé, outright pace wasn't important, but the balance of the chassis and having the right amount of grip to balance the power and the brakes was. The result is a fantastic, fun, driver's car. It won't set lap records around the 'Ring, but it will guarantee the driver has a smile on his/her face after each lap. So, bear in mind that the chase for ultimate power or lap times isn't necessarily going to give you a better day at the track.

The next few chapters will look at a variety of modifications and developments you can make to your car. Whilst they are in no particular order, they do follow a pattern of the modifications with the best 'value' to the project. The chapters are loosely split along the lines of cheap, medium and expensive modifications, but within each will be a description of not only what to do, but also why it benefits the project as a whole. Generally, you would find it best to follow the modifications in pretty much the order they're presented in the book, especially if you're doing it over time rather than as one complete strip and build job. Having said that, there's nothing stopping you cherry picking certain modifications and ignoring others. I'll explain the relative importance of each modification to give you an idea of the best path to follow with your chosen track weapon. I won't give too many specific details on the actual work to be done, though, as this will vary a lot from car to car. However, once you've got an idea of the job you want to do, it's often then best to consult a workshop manual for the exact technical process to follow.

Let's start with the most cost-effective upgrades. Great track manners, speed and enjoyment can be had for very little money.

WEIGHT

Weight is the enemy of performance. For a graphic example of this, try sprinting from one end of your garden to the other, turn around at the far end, then sprint back. Now, try it again whilst giving a friend a piggy-back ride. It's much harder the second time around. Adding the extra weight makes it harder to accelerate from a standstill, more difficult to get anywhere near your top sprinting speed, requires you to slow down earlier as your momentum is greater, makes it harder to turn around, etc. The more weight you can shed from your car the better. It will make you quicker, whilst also saving wear and tear on the tyres, brakes, clutch, suspension bushes, etc. At a basic level, make sure you take out the spare wheel before you go on track, along with any jack or toolkit in the car, plus your bag, coats, and any rubbish in the door pockets and glovebox. Don't carry any drinks cans/bottles in the car on the track. Fluids weigh a lot, and, if the containers come loose, could potentially roll under the brake pedal as you approach a hairpin at speed.

More drastic measures include removing the rear seats. These are usually held in by a couple of bolts at

Stripped interior. (Author collection)

the front and back, so are quite easy to remove. Next, take out all the carpet. This is usually glued in place, but can be teased out with a little gentle persuasion. You might as well take out any centre console or lower dash trim pieces as well, as they're just there for show. Although the plastic bits won't weigh much, every little helps. It's also worth going for the trim panels on the doors (known as the door cards), and below the rear side windows on a two-door car. Since you have to run most trackdays with the windows closed, it's worth getting rid of cumbersome electric window mechanisms. Once you've removed the door cards, it's

worth cutting some plastic or thin aluminium sheet to cover the inner door area. There are quite a few holes and sharp edges on the inside of the door, so it's best to cover these with a sheet of material to avoid catching yourself on them, especially in the event of an accident. Remember to cut holes for the door handle and window winding mechanisms, though.

It's worth keeping two seats in the front: you'll no doubt want to take your mates out in the car at some point, and, if you plan on getting some track driving coaching, the instructor will need somewhere to sit. Road car seats tend to be very heavy. They are usually very

well padded and sprung for comfort, and have adjustment mechanisms for fore and aft and up and down movement, tilting, etc. Electrically-adjusted seats have heavy motors as well. If the original seats are on runners, you can usually release a catch on the runners then slide off the seats (which means you can get to all the adjustment mechanisms and mounts below). Good quality race or track seats can be had for relatively little money, and can be mounted directly to the floor (it's best to weld on some mounts or use a sandwich of 3mm thick steel plates, 60mm x 60mm, to bolt through and sandwich the vehicle floor in-between) or the original mounting points. As you're going to be the only driver you don't need to worry about adjustment; just get it set up for what you find comfortable, then bolt it into position (see Chapter 2, Rule 1 for guidance on where to position the seat). The other advantage of these types of seat is they are very good at holding you in place. The high-sided bucket shape holds your body more securely through the corners, and is much better than a normal (or even sports) road seat, which makes driving, and feeling the response of the car, much easier.

So far, stripping weight hasn't cost anything other than time (unless you decided to go for the racing seat option). You might even have made a little money if you managed to sell any of your surplus items. With all that money you've saved/made, it's worth getting hold of a heat gun, as the next job will be to get rid of the soundproofing material (the sticky tar-like substance which cakes the floor and centre tunnel). Heat it vigorously with the heat gun, and use a metal wallpaper scraper to peel it off. It's a time-consuming, hot and dull job, but the reward is a gleaming clean interior. One word of warning, though: keep an eye on where the heat gun is pointing, as it's very easy to burn yourself (and any wiring routed through the car). Once you've finished the inside, it's time to get the car up in the air (on a two-post rig if you have access to one, as this will make life much easier; if not, then axle stands will do the job), and, with your trusty heat gun and scraper, start working on the rust-proofing underseal. This makes stripping away the gunk inside the car look easy, but be prepared for a long job.

The last major weight-saving job is the glass. You can save a lot of weight (and weight mounted high up in the car), by replacing the glass with a minimum of 4mm thick plastic. The side windows on the car will be relatively easy, as they generally only curve in one direction, so you can purchase the plastic from your local DIY store and cut it to shape. Use the existing glass as a pattern, and secure the new plastic screen in place using the existing rubber mounts (on older cars), or make up some small

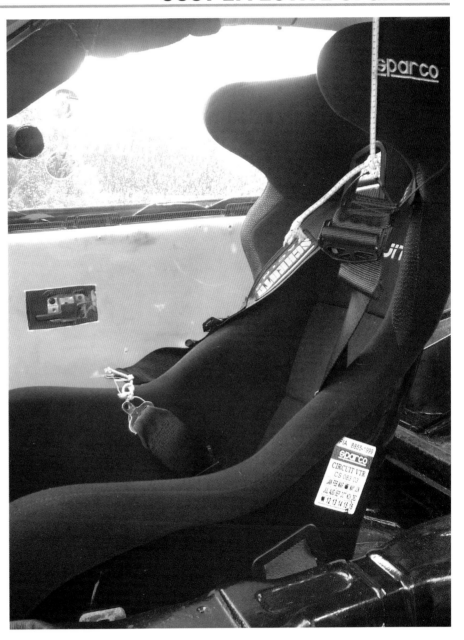

Race seat. (Author collection)

steel or aluminium brackets to hold the window in place, and use silicone sealant to make a watertight seal around the mounting face. Front and rear screens will be more difficult to make, but you may find a company out there who either already makes them or is able to.

For the driver and passenger windows, it can be worth using a tank cutter attachment on a drill to cut some ventilation holes.

When you're finished, it's always a good idea to weigh everything you've removed from the car. A lot of the stuff feels light when you're removing it, but it all adds up to quite a bit. It's always a morale boost to see the actual kilograms removed after a long evening of scuffed knuckles and swearing.

Plastic windows help reduce weight. (Author collection)

BRAKES

The first thing you need to do when trying to go faster around a circuit is improve stopping. It may sound perverse, but the more efficient the braking is, and the longer the brakes can last at track pace, the faster you will be overall. This is because you'll be using them for less time, so will be on the power longer, and you won't need to compromise your driving (such as by lifting off earlier on the straights to reduce the speed before using the brakes, so they don't get too hot). Even if you've stripped all of the weight out of the car as described earlier, the road brakes won't be up to the job of

repeated heavy braking. The brakes on your road car have been designed to work from cold and only be used heavily in emergency situations. Repeated heavy braking, like you will be doing on a trackday, will lead to brake fade problems very quickly, sometimes even within just a few corners.

The first, and most cost-effective upgrades you should look at are changing the brake pad compound and the brake fluid.

There are a variety of competition, or 'fast road' brake pads on the market, catering for all price points. Regardless of how much you can spend, any of the available brands will offer an

improvement over the standard pads in your car. Even pads at the cheaper end of the market, such as EBC, offer a distinct performance advantage, both in out-and-out stopping power and in endurance, but the further up the price ladder you go, to manufacturers such as Performance Friction, the more performance benefits you will see. The uprated pads will not only work better out on the track, but they are generally more resistant to heat, so they're less likely to break up after repeated heat cycles. What you will also find is that each manufacturer builds the pad using different materials, and in different percentages and mixtures, so they will

Uprated pads assist stopping performance and efficiency. (Author collection)

performance and heat dissipation. It can also be worth experimenting with different disk manufacturers, as some disks will be better than others. Some manufacturers can even supply uprated disks with better cooling or heat dissipation.

Once you have the pads sorted, it's also worth changing the brake fluid to a competition version. Standard brake fluid is designed for the everyday driving and braking conditions we spoke about earlier: immediate responsiveness from cold, and occasional high-performance requirement in an emergency situation. Repeated heavy braking will cause the fluid to overheat, and it will literally boil in the cylinders and the lines. This boiling leads to vaporisation of the fluid, whereupon it loses its hydraulic qualities. This is when you start to experience the spongy pedal feeling of hard-worked brakes. Higher specification brake fluids (referred to as DOT 4, DOT 5.1 or Competition/Racing brake fluid) have a much higher boiling point, so are less prone to this vaporisation.

When flushing out the old fluid and replacing it with new, it's definitely best to have two people on the job, one to keep pressing the pedal, and one to tighten and release the bleed nipple and top-up the fluid in the master cylinder.

all give a different brake pedal 'feel.' It is, therefore, worth experimenting with different types of pad, if you have the time and the budget, to get to a solution which is not only gives you the performance you want but also the brake 'feel' that you like.

When you change from one manufacturer of pad to another, it's important to clean the brake disk thoroughly with brake cleaner, to rid the disk surface of the chemical compounds from the previous pad. Without doing this you may find the new pad doesn't bite very well, as it has to clean the disk surface first before it can bed in. Spray-on brake cleaner can be sourced from most motor factors and vehicle parts supply stores. Alternatively, you can go for a replacement disk. A new disk will have more 'meat' on the braking surface, which will help with stopping

Performance disk and pad setup.
(Author collection)

Getting a brake caliper too hot can have disastrous consequences, like melting brake pads! (Author collection)

Uprated brake fluid will be less inclined to boil at high temperatures.
(Author collection)

There are 'one-man' kits available on the market, but they are generally more trouble than they are worth.

DOT 5 brake fluid is not glycol-based like all other fluids, it's a silicone-based fluid, which can only really be specified in a brand new system, and only on non-ABS cars. It has qualities which don't react well to existing glycol or moisture in the system. The silicone doesn't absorb moisture (making it effectively a maintenance-free fluid), but if there's any moisture in the system already (even small amounts trapped in the remnants of glycol-based fluid left behind) the hydraulic quality of the fluid will be reduced, and corrosion of components may occur.

A good DOT 4 or DOT 5.1 fluid, such as the Performance Friction 665 Racing Fluid or the AP 551 Racing Brake Fluid, will suffice in most situations.

Whilst you're changing the fluid, it's also worth changing the flexible hoses for braided ones. The flexible hose is the part of the brake hose between the solid metal tube running from the master cylinder to the wheelarch, and which is fixed to the car body, and the caliper itself. It needs to be flexible to be able to move with the suspension movements and steering of the car. These hoses will, on a road car, be made of rubber, which is fine for everyday driving, but when the fluid and caliper heat up to the extreme temperatures generated on track, the rubber will become softer and more pliable. This might sound like a good

Braided brake hose. (Author collection)

action and contributes to a spongy or vague pedal feel.

A braided brake hose has an inner hose (the part carrying the fluid) of Teflon or PTFE, rather than the rubber of a standard hose, surrounded by an outer hose made of interwoven steel fibres. These two elements combined are much more resistant to expansion, whilst still offering flexibility along their length to compensate for wheel movements relative to the chassis of the car. Flexible hoses are usually available in kits of four hoses, cost relatively little money, and bring a performance benefit far outweighing the small cost. Packs of hoses are usually available tailored to specific models of car, and will be cut to the right lengths with the right connectors on each end for joining the flexible hose to the main (solid) brake line at one end, and the caliper assembly at the other. If you're unable to find a kit, it's relatively easy to make the hoses from the component parts, or you can ask your local mechanic to do it.

One last brake mod to consider is that of brake cooling. This can be as simple as a section of flexible hose, cable-tied to the lower arm of the suspension, which draws air from under the car and forces it into the disk and caliper area. The most effective way of capturing the air is to cut a hole in the bumper or front valance, and duct the air directly from the front of the car. This will be the least disturbed air, so will be as cool and as dense as possible. If it's possible to make or modify the backplate of the disc to funnel air into the disk directly, then that will also be a great benefit.

thing, but what it means is that when you press the brake pedal the high pressure of the hydraulic brake fluid will be able to stretch the hose to a small degree, making it bulge out. This increases the internal volume of the hose and hence reduces the force of fluid acting on the caliper. This gives reduced braking

Chapter 5
Spending some money

It's now time to look at some bolt-on parts that will make your car go faster. All the items discussed here are readily available in the large aftermarket tuning world, and most are accompanied by a lot of advertising information (and misinformation), which can make choosing the right part on the right budget a bit of a minefield.

Now that we've made the car lighter and better at stopping, we'll look at the cornering potential and how we can improve it.

WHEELS AND TYRES

The defining factor to how much grip your car has going around a bend is how much rubber it has connecting it to the tarmac. It stands to reason, then, that the more rubber there is the more grip there'll be. However, before you rush out and buy the widest wheels and tyres your budget will support, make sure they will fit (and the ways they might not are many and varied).

First, there will be a limit to how wide you can go. Make sure the wheel fits within the maximum widths for the car. You may find, for example, that the front wheel is narrower than the back, because it has to turn, and so requires

Lighter alloy wheel. (Author collection)

extra clearance which may not be possible with excessively wide tyres. If you have run out of space inside the wheelarch, you can extend the wheel beyond the original bodywork, but it's important to fit wheelarch extensions over the protruding wheel and tyre, especially if you're going to drive the car on the road, as this is a legal requirement in most countries. Likewise, many trackday operators don't like exposed wheels and tyres, because of the extra risks they bring in the unlikely event of car-to-car contact on track. Furthermore, bear in mind that the tyre may foul the original bodywork when the suspension is compressed, so this may need to be cut out of the way if the wheelarch is being extended.

The width of the wheel will be advertised with a nominal value, traditionally in inches; this is to get around the situations where a wheel is made up of a mixture of metric and imperial measurements. Hence, an 8in

wide wheel will now simply be advertised as a width of 8. Often, you will see a letter after the wheel width, usually a J. This simply refers to the shape of the tyre bead (the contact area between the rim and the tyre), and references a code for tyre and wheel manufacturers to match up their tyres and wheels.

Second, you need to make sure the bolt pattern of the wheel hub is available in the wheel you want. The bolt pattern and dimensions are known as the PCD, the Pitch Circle Diameter (also known as the BCD or Bolt Circle Diameter). A PCD can be listed in inches or millimetres, and will be presented like 5/130 or 5x130. This would be a five-bolt pattern with a diameter of 130mm (5.12in).

The next thing to look at is the

offset. This is the distance from the centre line of the wheel to the mounting face, and will be listed as a plus or minus number. The smaller the number the further out the wheel will sit. It's always best to stay within the car manufacturer's tolerances, as increasing the distance the wheel sits from the car affects not only the steering and suspension geometry, but also the thrust load on the wheel bearings, as the wheel will effectively act like a longer lever.

Once the offset is sorted, check the centre bore. A wheel will be known as either Hub-Centric or Lug-Centric. A hub-centric wheel will need to have a centre bore dimension identical to the mounting hub of the car (or have a spacer or adapter to make up the

Wheel with sticky track tyre fitted. (Author collection)

difference). A hub-centric wheel uses this centre bore to centre the wheel when mounting, and take some of the vertical loads off the lug nuts. A lug-centric wheel will use tapered lug nuts and a tapered socket on the wheel to centre them correctly. In this instance, the centre bore must simply be larger than the mounting hub of the car.

Finally, you need to check that the inside diameter of the wheel will clear your caliper and mount.

Once you've determined all of those factors, you'll need to decide on the size of wheel you want. You could stick with the original wheel diameter; though, of course, it might be worth going bigger, or even smaller. A larger diameter wheel will give you a lower profile tyre sidewall for the same rolling radius. This will have a beneficial effect on the handling of the car. As the car turns through a corner the flexible sidewall will be able to bend, meaning the wheel and the tyre are sitting at slightly different angles. This dulls the steering response, and too much flex can cause the tyre to start to 'tuck-under' so only the outer shoulder of the tyre is contacting the tarmac. A shorter sidewall will allow less flex, improving the steering response and cornering grip. A smaller wheel will be lighter, allowing for slightly greater acceleration and top speed (and better fuel economy if that's of any interest), but it also allows you to run a smaller tyre than was originally fitted to the car – this helps the sidewall flex detailed above, but also reduces the rolling diameter of the tyre (increasing acceleration), and the ride height (lowering the centre of gravity for better cornering).

Tyres are the next thing on the list. Once you've decided whether you're going larger or smaller with regard to your wheel size, you can pick a tyre size. Tyres will be sized in the following format 285/30 R18 93Z. To decipher this we just need to split it into its separate parts:

285 – The width of the tyre in mm.
30 – The profile of the sidewall of the tyre measured as a percentage of the tyre width (ie, this is 30% of 285).
R – Radial construction.
18 – The diameter of the wheel rim, stated as a nominal figure but measured in inches (just to confuse metric and imperial measurements).

93 – The load capacity of the tyre. The number refers to a load rating table where 93 is equivalent to 650kg or 1400lb of load on that tyre.
Z – The speed rating of the tyre. Z is a high-performance tyre rated for use on cars capable of a top speed of over 149mph or 240kph.

Make sure the tyre you're fitting has an equal or higher load and speed rating than the manufacturer recommendation.

Trackday tyres are a relatively new phenomenon. 15 years ago they hadn't even been thought of, but these days most tyre manufacturers produce a track-biased tyre of some description. These are produced with a much softer compound than normal road tyres, much closer to a full slick racing tyre, but they have a few grooves cut into them; just enough to be road legal.

These tyres are what is referred to as 'dry-bias' tyres, in that they are designed to work best in dry conditions on a good road surface (like a race track). They generally still work quite well in damp conditions, as long as you can keep heat in the tyres, but they do struggle with standing water as the small number of grooves don't dissipate the water quickly enough. The popular brands are the Toyo R888, Yokohama A048, and the Dunlop Direzza DZ03, but there are tyres from all the major manufacturers in budgets to suit all tastes. Quite often, you'll be able to get these tyres in different compounds as well. As a guide, the softest tyre will give you outright lap pace, whereas a harder compound will keep a good level of performance all day long. However, this is affected by a number of factors, so there's no hard-and-fast rule. A heavier car will work its tyres harder, so might need a harder compound to avoid overheating and going off. A cold day might mean a harder tyre won't be able to generate enough heat, especially in a light car, so a softer tyre might be needed. The best thing to do is either ask someone with a similar car what they run, ask the manufacturer or retailer if they can offer advice, or, failing that, pick a middle or medium compound to start with and you'll see if you need to go softer or harder after your first day on track.

SUSPENSION

If you've been implementing each of these upgrades in turn, you'll now have a pretty fast track car, but one that may be a little compromised in the corners. The standard road suspension will be a bit soft for track use, especially on an older car, and even your stripped-out, lightweight track machine will be a little too much for the springs and dampers to cope with. You'll find the car will dive a lot under heavy braking, wallow over onto its side in the corners, then squat down and push wide on the throttle out of the corners. Also, this all happens quite slowly, the large range of movement of the suspension and the soft springs and dampers means the car rolls about in a relatively slow manner. This makes it easy to control, but the responsiveness of the chassis is dulled considerably, and it will be difficult to change direction quickly – in a chicane, for example.

Replacing the stock components with shorter and stiffer springs and firmer dampers will have a dramatic effect on the car. Shorter springs will lower the ride height. Initially, you'd assume that lowering the car also lowers the centre-of-gravity, and that the lower this is, the flatter the car will stay through a corner. The centre of gravity is, in a simple explanation, the balance point of the car. The lower it is the less it is affected during manoeuvres, such as cornering. However, lowering the roll centre has a greater effect. By lowering the car you change the angle of the suspension geometry. When this changes, it (in most cases), lowers the roll centre of the car. The roll centre is a point in space about which the car pivots when it rolls to the left and right on its suspension. Lowering the suspension and changing the angle of the suspension arms will move the roll centre further than it moves the centre of gravity, and it's the relationship between the two that determines the amount of roll the car will be subject to under a given load.

So, by lowering the suspension, the roll centre has moved away from the centre of gravity, increasing the effective lever arm length between the two points, and, therefore, giving it more inclination to roll under the same given load. You can think of it like an upside down pendulum. If you hold the pendulum near the weight at the top as you tip it to

Stiffer springs and a lower ride height achieved by changing suspension components. (Author collection)

Adjustable suspension mounted on the car. (Author collection)

one side, it's fairly stable, the weight will roll to the side but it is relatively easy to control, and the amount it moves is not too large. If you hold the pendulum near the bottom, at the point furthest from the weight, and do the same exercise, it's much less stable, and will more easily roll to the side and fall, whilst physically moving a larger distance.

So why lower the car at all? Well, it's like taking one step back to take two forward. By lowering the car you do benefit from a slightly lower centre of gravity, which allows you to change direction a bit more easily, and, more importantly, reduces dive and squat. Running stiffer springs and shocks with less travel allows the car to move about less, and controls the weight distribution better. The increased inclination to roll can be controlled

A complete ARB showing the adjustment holes at the end. (Author collection)

ARB connector shown (disconnected) with three mount points for adjustment of the roll amount. (Author collection)

in most instances by running a stiffer Anti-Roll Bar (ARB). The ARB is a type of torsion spring fixed to the wheel end of the suspension arm of the left- and right-hand wheels, and also mounted to the chassis of the car. As the car tries to roll in a corner, the suspension being compressed pulls up its end of the ARB. This twisting force is transferred along the length of the ARB to the opposite wheel which is also pulled upwards. This has the effect of reducing the droop (or rebound) of the suspension on the wheel on the inside of the corner, effectively pulling down the body of the car, and making it flatter. I mentioned this will only work to a certain extent, and this is because if the roll centre is moved too far from the centre of gravity, the ARB cannot do enough to control the body of the car, and the inside wheels will leave the ground.

The issue of roll centres generally has less impact on more modern cars than it does on older cars. Modern suspension design allows for a more compliant ride with less suspension travel, so newer cars will generally have a reduced overall range of motion in the suspension. This also means, however, that there will be a reduced scope for lowering (both available and required) in a more modern car, so the angle of the suspension changes less dramatically, and the roll centre moves less.

When fitting stiffer ARBs, you can often replace the original items with adjustable ones. An adjustable anti-roll bar will have a range of mounting points at the ends of the arms for connecting to the suspension. Using the mounting points at the ends of the arm will give a longer lever effect, which has the effect of reducing the resistance to the bar twisting, whereas using the mounting point furthest from the end reduces the lever length, thus increasing the resistance to twisting and giving a stiffer bar and less roll.

With the car fitted with stiffer springs and dampers, dive, squat and roll when braking, accelerating and cornering will all be reduced. The car will be flatter in the corners, and more responsive. Grip will also increase as the tyres will be able to work more effectively.

If the car is rolling around on its stock suspension, then, mid-corner the

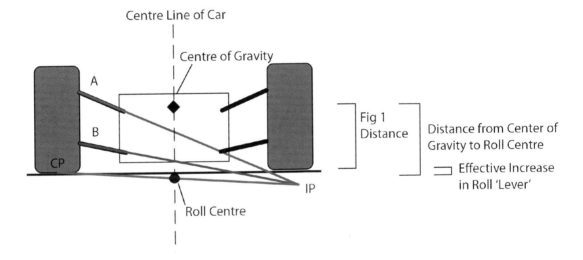

The roll centre is defined by drawing a line from the intersection point (IP) of the angle of the suspension arms (A and B) back to the Contact Patch of the tyre (CP) Where this line crosses the vertical line defined by the Center of Gravity of the car is the roll centre.

As we can see by moving from Fig 1 to Fig 2, lowering the suspension alters the angle of the suspension arms which moves the Roll Centre further away from the Centre of Gravity thereby increasing the 'lever' effect of the Centre of Gravity on the Roll Centre which is the point at which the car rolls about (pivot or fulcrum). Purpose built race cars will move the points where the suspension attaches to the chassis to be able to run the arms more parallel and hence bring the Roll Centre and Centre of Gravity closer together, reducing the induced body roll.

Roll centre and centre of gravity. (Author collection)

Adjustment knob mounted on the top of the strut. (Author collection)

car will have a greater angle of lean. This will have a direct bearing on the angle of the tyre touching the road, and there will be less of the surface of the tyre in contact with the ground (it will be riding more on the shoulder. As we saw above, more rubber on the road equals more grip, so by keeping the car flatter in the corner the tyre stays flatter and more of the surface of the tyre will be on the road.

The other reason you will have more grip with stiffer springs and dampers is that the weight distribution of the car will be more even across its wheels. Again, looking at the car with standard suspension, as you accelerate out of a right-hand bend, for example, the body is able to roll around on its springs; it will be rolling to the left-hand side and squatting to the rear in this instance. This means that more of the overall weight of the car is being carried on the left rear tyre, and hardly any is on the right front. If you have stiffer springs and dampers, however, the chassis of the car cannot move around so much, so less of the weight is transferred to the left rear and more is kept on the right front. This better balances the workload of the tyres, so they are each less likely to lose traction. The knock-on benefit is

that your tyres will last longer, as they are rolling onto their edges less, and each tyre isn't going through such a dramatic cycle of loadings and work.

Many companies, such as GAZ Shocks, Bilstein, KW Suspension, or Eibach, offer kits for specific cars. The springs and dampers (generally fairly easy 'plug and play' affairs), will be matched to the car and each other, and you can usually choose from fast road through to full race spec setups. The higher spec kits often also allow for ride height control and variable damping stiffness, so you can fine-tune the handling of your car. The variable

A soft car cornering. (Courtesy David Stallard)

A stiffer car cornering. (Courtesy David Stallard)

damping systems are often termed as one-, two-, three-, four- or multiple-way dampers. Each 'way' refers to the control of a particular aspect of the damping.

To look at these different types, let's first look at how a damper works. The damper's main job is to 'dampen' the movement of the spring during compression and expansion (rebound). This is done by moving fluid from one end of the damper to the other as it compresses or rebounds. Adjusting the stiffness of the damper is achieved by increasing or decreasing the rate of flow of the fluid, making it easier or more difficult for the damper to compress and rebound.

One-way adjustable dampers – These usually allow you to adjust both the compression and the rebound of the damper by the same amount, or just the rebound (the speed at which it returns the spring to its natural state). This can help stabilise the weight distribution of a car going into or out of a corner. By increasing the rebound stiffness of the front dampers, for example, they will take longer to return to neutral after being compressed, so they'll 'hold' the weight of the front of the car over the front tyres slightly longer after releasing the brakes to allow for more grip on turn-in.
Two-way adjustable dampers – These allow for separate adjustment of both the compression and the rebound, allowing better tuning of the handling of the car into, through, and out of the corners.
Three-way adjustable dampers – These generally allow for the adjustment of the rebound, whilst splitting the compression adjustment into slow-speed and high-speed. This opens up a whole new range of fine-tuning possibilities: low-speed adjustment controls the weight distribution and body control, whilst high-speed adjustment controls the way the damper reacts to bumps and road surface imperfections.
Four-way adjustable damper – These allow for adjustment of high- and low-speed compression, and high- and low-speed rebound.

The ride height is adjusted via the spring mounts on the damper body, and the stiffness is altered via a knob on the damper, which increases or reduces the oil flow from one end of the damper to the other.

A direct comparison of a stiffer car and a softer car in the same corner showing the extra roll induced by softer suspension. (Courtesy David Stallard)

Suspension becomes less easy to tune or develop in cars with torsion bar setups, as there are fewer suppliers providing alternative spring rates as kit parts. It's easier for these companies to provide you with a kit which converts a torsion bar setup to a coil spring setup. Torsion bars are actually a great bit of design. From a manufacturer's point of view, they offer a sprung suspension system within a lot less space than a traditional coil spring, and for the tuner they can be relatively easy to adjust. Ride height, for example, can be adjusted by rotating the bar on one end or the other of its splines.

To get a basic height setup on the car, it's a good idea to take out the torsion bars on both sides. Lay them on the ground parallel to one another, with the inner and outer ends together. Make sure both are sitting on the same splines at each end (usually there will be a different number of splines at each end to allow for fine-tuning the ride height), and mark the top spline on the outer face of each of the bars. Slot them both back into place, keeping the marked top outer spline pointing straight up. You should then be able to mount the hub assembly on each side in the same relative position to give an equal ride height across the car. You can then fine-tune this using the adjustment bolts on the hub and trailing arm assembly.

When removing the original coil springs from the car you may need to use a spring compressor to squeeze the springs enough to get them off their mounting plates. The new, shorter springs will be easier to put back, as they'll probably be shorter than the total droop of the suspension system: however, in some cases, you may need the compressor to assist fitting. If your new springs are considerably shorter than the droop in the suspension, keep a close eye on them whenever you jack up and lower the car to make sure they seat correctly.

Stiffer suspension will increase grip and responsiveness, but at the cost of making the car harder to drive. As the springs, dampers and ARBs are stiffer, they'll move the weight around much more quickly. This is the improved responsiveness that you will like in the handling of the car. However, once the car breaks traction, it will do it more quickly and with less warning, so you'll need to be more focused to stay in control. For a graphic example of this take a look on the internet at a couple of onboard cameras from different cars on the same track, such as a Nascar and an Indycar around Infineon Raceway

Intake (blue filter on the right of the shot) shielded from the heat of the engine bay to allow it to draw in cooler, and hence denser, air. (Author collection)

(Sears Point) in America. You'll see the Indycar driver will be moving the wheel much more quickly to correct the car over bumps and during slides, whereas the Nascar driver, with a softer setup, will roll more and slide more, but their input and reactions to the car are slower, as everything the car does happens more slowly (just like your car did on its standard, soft suspension).

INTAKE MODIFICATIONS

Your car will produce power (assuming it's powered by an internal combustion engine), by mixing fuel with air in the right quantity, and then igniting it to create an explosion which moves the piston down and turns the crankshaft. The size of the explosion is determined by how much air and fuel is put into the cylinder before it's ignited. You can adjust the available mixture by modifying the inlet of your engine. The car will automatically increase the amount of fuel injected based on the air being supplied; so, to modify the intake, you're looking at increasing the airflow into the engine.

Starting at the intake, let's look at the air filter. Contrary to most marketing, a 'performance' air filter doesn't really make any difference over a standard one. Maybe 1 or 2bhp, but nothing dramatic.

However, it's always worth changing, as a performance filter will generally be easier to maintain. What can be of benefit, though, is the quality of the air being supplied to the filter. The cooler the air is, the denser it is, and the more oxygen it contains (oxygen being required to ignite with the fuel). If possible, shroud the air intake from the rest of the engine bay, so it draws in cooler air from outside rather than the warm under-bonnet air in the engine bay. This can help increase the 'bang' in the cylinder. Also, creating an air duct from the front of the car which forces cool air into the air intake, especially at speed, increases the volume of air being

Larger exhaust to more easily draw out exhaust gasses. (Author collection)

pushed through the engine. This is the concept behind the 'Ram-Air' bonnets you would see on muscle cars in the '70s, and the large air intake above the driver's head on a Formula 1 car. Although it doesn't make a great difference until you get to some pretty high speeds, it might help a little.

Moving back from the filter and the intake we arrive at the throttle body. This is the part which is directly connected to the throttle pedal, via a cable or electronics, and as you press the pedal a valve opens inside the throttle body allowing more air into the engine. The engine's ECU recognises this by measuring the airflow with a sensor, and

provides the corresponding amount of fuel to the cylinder to keep the fuel:air ratio perfect for combustion. Increasing the size and/or action of the valve will allow more air to pass for any given throttle input, compensated by more fuel from the engine and a bigger bang resulting in more power. Larger throttle bodies can usually be bought off-the-shelf for different models of car, and it's a simple job to unbolt the old one and replace with the new one. Some cars may require a retune following this, to recognise the extra air, or a change of the Mass Airflow Sensor (MAF) – this is the sensor used by the ECU to measure the amount of air coming into the engine.

EXHAUST MODIFICATIONS
All of that air you've just put into the engine needs to get out again. If the exhaust system is in any way restricting the escape of the exhaust gases, you'll get what is referred to as 'back-pressure,' where the escaping gasses are met by the previous pulse of escaping gasses before they've had time to get out of the exhaust. This pressure builds and effectively causes a blockage in the system which prevents the engine from running efficiently. Using an exhaust with a bigger bore and smoother manifold ports will allow the gasses to escape easier, and will reduce the back-pressure. Bigger isn't always

Some cars come with a fairly large exhaust already ... (Author collection)

better, though. A normally-aspirated engine will need a certain amount of back-pressure to operate at its peak, whereas a turbocharged engine will need to get rid of as much gas as possible as quickly as possible. So, a normally-aspirated engine will have an optimum exhaust configuration which is smaller than that of a turbo car. Bear in mind as well that the larger the exhaust (and the more items in the exhaust you might have removed to reduce the back-pressure, such as silencers and catalytic converters), the louder the exhaust will be, and that might get you into trouble with the 'noise police' on the trackday.

ECU MODIFICATIONS

More modern cars which use an ECU (Electronic Control Unit) to run their engine are the easiest of all to tune. Unlike older engines, a newer one will be built with far better tolerances, and the design of the ports, etc, will be optimised to allow the engine to run as efficiently as possible. This effectively renders a lot of traditional engine tuning redundant, unless you're going for an extreme performance overhaul, but for the trackday driver it means you can get the best from your engine without getting oil under your nails! The ECU in your car will have a program on it which runs all the important aspects of the engine; from fuel:air mixtures to spark timing and variable cam timing, etc. This program will be written to provide a good level of economy and a good level of performance, whilst keeping everything within manufacturing tolerances, meeting emissions and noise regulations, etc. A specialist ECU tuning company can unlock the potential of your engine by installing a new program which makes sure everything on the engine runs to its optimum. This can yield significant performance advantages in return for a few minutes with the car plugged into a laptop. If you want to use your car on the road and don't want any issues with insurance companies, it's relatively easy on most cars to have a second ECU, one with the standard factory program, and a 'trackday' ECU with the optimal tune program. Swapping them over is usually as simple as undoing a few clips and unplugging a few cables.

VISIT VELOCE ON THE WEB – WWW.VELOCE.CO.UK
All current books • New book news • Special offers • Gift vouchers • Forum

Chapter 6
Dedicated trackday car

Now you've got this far you might as well go the whole hog, eh? In this chapter, we'll be looking at taking the car to the extreme: an ultimate trackday toy with no regard for everyday usability and practicality!

INTERIOR
Having gotten this far we'll assume you've done most if not all of the modifications previously talked about in this book. If so, then one of the first things you did to your car was to strip out all of the unnecessary weight to give it a better power-to-weight ratio. What we're going to do now is put a load of weight back in! This sounds a bit contradictory, but there are two main reasons for this: safety and rigidity.

Roll cage
The first thing we're going to look at is installing a roll cage. More than just a collection of old scaffolding, roll cages are designed with two purposes. First, and arguably the most important, they are there for safety. In the, hopefully unlikely, event of an accident, the roll cage will provide an extra layer of strength to the bodyshell of the car, whilst cocooning you inside in a relatively

A roll cage will aid chassis stiffness and keep you safe. (Author collection)

The bright orange belts anchored at the correct angles. (Author collection)

safe location. If the car were to roll over, the bars above your head will stop the roof from caving in, giving you a precious survival bubble in the car. Second, the cage will make the chassis more rigid, and thus less able to flex as the car brakes, accelerates and corners. If the chassis were to flex, of course, it would alter the suspension geometry and affect the finely-balanced handling you worked hard to set up.

The chassis doesn't have to flex much for it to affect the driving experience. If you think about a convertible car compared to its coupé or saloon twin, the hard-topped version will be a much more enjoyable car to chuck around, as it will feel a bit more responsive to the steering, and a bit more direct and 'planted' in the corners. This is due to the extra stiffness derived from the roof. With regard to your trackday car, pushing it hard in the corners will put a lot of twisting forces through the chassis, with the stiffer suspension (having less give and compliance in the springs and dampers), transferring more of this torsional force to the body itself. By connecting the roll cage to numerous points on the car, you'll have the effect of triangulating the shell, bracing and supporting it, making it more rigid. As well as the feet of the cage, which will be welded to the floor, you should look at connecting the cage to the 'A' pillars (windscreen surround), possibly the 'B' pillars (back of the front doors), and, if you can get to them, the front and rear shock absorber mounts. If you can also add strut braces between the tops of the front and rear shock absorbers, you'll add a further level of support and bracing for the chassis.

Seatbelts

Once you have the cage installed, it's time to get some proper belts as well. Belts, or harnesses, are not only there to keep you in place in the event of an accident, but they also support your body as you brake, accelerate and corner. The G-forces you can expect to achieve from your car now that it's lighter, running on stickier tyres, and with better suspension, will be far greater than those you experience on the road, and you'll be experiencing those forces much more regularly; every few seconds as the next corner is dealt with. Although more awkward, I would always suggest getting a five- or six-point harness, rather than just a four-point one. The number of 'points' refers to the number of anchor points on the car. A four-point harness has two shoulder straps and two lap straps buckled together in the middle of your hips. A five- or six-point harness has one or two additional straps anchored to the floor under the seat, and coming up between your legs to meet the same buckle. These extra straps will reduce the chances of you sliding under the belts in the event of a frontal impact, whilst also keeping the lap straps low to avoid the belts lifting in the event of an impact. Pay particular attention to the position of the anchor points on the chassis, and the angle of the belts. In an impact, the belts can potentially do you more damage than good if they do not have 'hard points' of your body to brace. If the lap strap is pulled too high, for example, your body will move forward in an impact as the belt squashes into your stomach. By siting the belt as low as possible, it will brace your pelvis, keeping you in the correctly restrained position whilst supporting the weight of your body on your pelvis.

Lap straps should be angled at approximately 60 degrees down from horizontal, and anchored as close to the edge of the seat as possible, so the anchor points are only just wider than the width of the seat. This allows the lap strap to be as short as possible, and to pull only in a longitudinal direction in the event of an impact. It also means it stays low over the top of the thighs, and rests against the pelvis, as discussed above.

The crotch strap, or straps, should be routed vertically down from the buckle.

The shoulder straps should leave your shoulders either parallel to the ground or, at most, on a 20-degree slope down to the back of the car. Ideally, they should be anchored about 20cm (8in) from the back of the seat at most to avoid too much belt being allowed

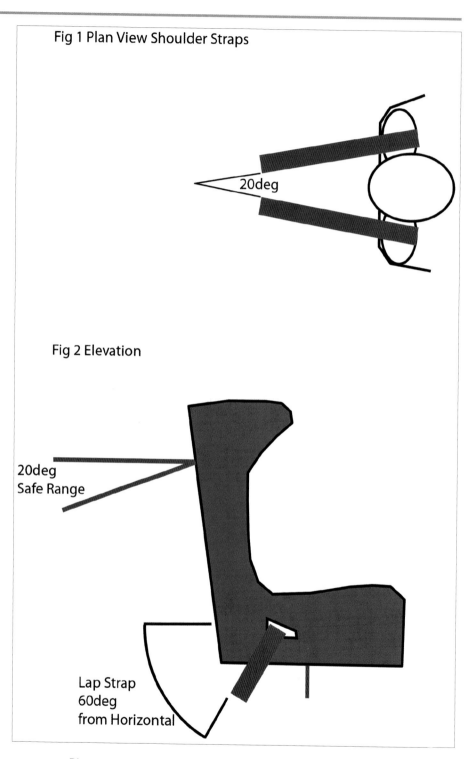

Fig 1 Plan View Shoulder Straps

20deg

Fig 2 Elevation

20deg
Safe Range

Lap Strap
60deg
from Horizontal

Diagrams showing the ideal harness alignment. (Author collection)

to stretch. Looking in plan view at the belts, they should be close together as they travel towards the anchor point. The angle between them should be

Uprated suspension bushes. (Courtesy Powerflex)

approximately 20 degrees. If the anchor point is far enough back, the belts may come together, or even cross over. The shoulder straps can be either anchored to the chassis via eye bolts, or can be wrapped around a horizontal roll cage bar. In the case of wrapping them around a bar, the adjustment slider should be positioned right up against the bar around which the belt is wrapped, and the belts should be secured to avoid them sliding along the bar.

For all the anchor points, if eye bolts are used, their mounting points to the chassis should be reinforced with 3mm thick steel plate placed on the back of the mounting point.

SUSPENSION

Having replaced the springs, dampers and anti-roll bars, the next steps are adding adjustment for the camber and caster settings, and replacing the rubber bushes with harder items. As you've no doubt seen, a lot of the

adjustments we've made so far involved making it stiffer or more solid. One of the main reasons for this is to improve the performance of the tyre and its contact patch on the road. By stiffening the suspension, you'll minimise body movement, which means it's easier to set the angle of the tyre so it's working at its optimum when loaded and going around a bend. Reducing 'play' or flex in the setup will keep the tyre pointing where you want, when you want. To help with this, it's worth swapping the factory suspension bushes for aftermarket performance items.

A suspension bush is a large rubber item that sits between the suspension and the chassis. It provides a flexible joint for the suspension arm, but its main purpose is to stop vibration travelling up the suspension arm and into the chassis, where it would be felt by the occupants. For performance driving comfort isn't an issue, so these items should be replaced by stiffer rubber or polyurethane items.

These will provide the flexibility that the bush requires, but not so much that it affects the tyre geometry. The downside is, as mentioned above, a reduction in ride quality – what chassis engineers refer to as NVH; Noise, Vibration and Harshness – but, out on a nice smooth racetrack, the benefits far outweigh any extra discomfort. On the road, however, these can quickly become wearing, as the extra noise and vibration felt in the car will tire you more quickly over a long distance.

We've mentioned the geometry of the wheel as it becomes loaded whilst cornering, and how, for track driving, the ideal position of the wheel will be different from the manufacturer's road-biased setup. On the road, the suspension will be set (usually to within fairly large tolerances) to have the wheels mostly as upright as possible, with a neutral or slightly toe-out stance. The upright angle of the wheel is the camber setting, and the 'toe' is the relative angle the wheels are pointing; ie, a neutral toe is with all four wheels pointing exactly straight ahead, and a toe-out angle is with the front of the tyres pointing away from each other.

Camber will have the most dramatic effect on the handling of the car, both from a comfort and a performance perspective. For performance requirements, you would ideally run with a fair amount of negative camber; this is where the top of the tyre leans in toward the center line of the car. This means that when you're loading the tyres in the corner, and the car is rolling on its suspension, the outer tyre rolls over onto the flat of the surface of the tyre, giving you the maximum contact patch, and hence grip.

For a road car, there are a couple of downsides to this setup, the first being increased and uneven tyre wear – because the tyres spend most of their time travelling in a straight line, the inner shoulder will wear very quickly. The second problem for a road car is that the tyre will tend to follow the angle of the road surface, so imperfections, dips, and cambers will interfere with the steering.

Most cars will have limited or even no adjustment for the camber settings, so it usually requires buying some form of 'kit' to give you more flexibility with the setup. The cheapest and simplest solution is to install camber bolts on the hubs, where they bolt onto the suspension arms. These eccentric bolts allow you to position the angle of the hub, or 'upright' accurately.

Alternatively, a camber plate can be installed on the top mount of the suspension or shock absorber tower. The camber plate has slotted holes in it to allow for the top mount to be moved in and out relative to the car, thus changing the camber angle. The exact camber required will vary from car-to-car, and will depend on such factors as tyre grip, vehicle weight, suspension, and ARB stiffness, etc. Generally speaking, in a rear-wheel drive car, the front and rear camber will ideally be more similar than in a front-wheel drive car. In the latter, you may use more negative camber on the rear to give the opposite effect from what we have seen above. If too much negative camber is introduced, the tyre will never roll quite fully onto its complete contact patch whilst cornering, thus reducing the available grip. A front-wheel drive car will generally understeer first (when the front tyres lose grip before the rears), so reducing the grip at the rear can balance the car. By fine-tuning the camber angle at the rear, you can have a stable car in fast corners, when the rear is evenly balanced and heavily loaded mid-turn, and a looser, or more oversteering car when the speeds are lower in tighter turns.

The amount of toe the car runs will also affect the handling, but to a lesser extent. A car with positive (in) toe will generally be more stable in a straight line, but to the slight detriment of tyre wear and straight line speed. Generally speaking, toe-in improves stability, but decreases steering response, and toe out increases steering response but decreases stability. On the driven wheels, the torque of acceleration can pull a wheel slightly forward changing the toe setting, so it can be worth bearing that in mind when setting up the car.

In general, a rear-wheel drive car will benefit from slight toe out at the front and neutral toe at the rear. This will give a good response on turn-in, but more stability under acceleration. By toeing out the rear too much, you'll increase the tendency to oversteer on the exit of the corner.

In a front-wheel drive car, you should look to add slight negative toe

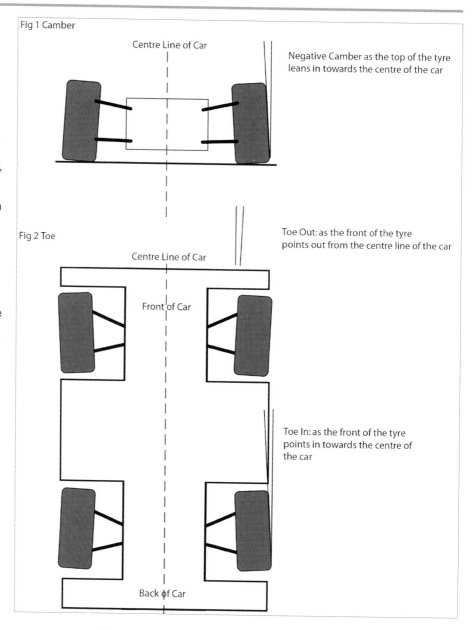

Diagrams showing camber and toe. (Author collection)

at the front, and the rear can often run quite dramatic toe out. This will reduce the natural understeer characteristic of a front-wheel drive car, ie, the rear of the car is happy to continue turning as the loaded tyre (on the outside), is pointing out of the corner, thus helping to pull around the back of the car.

ENGINE

With regard to the engine, we've already looked at improving the volume and flow of the air going in and out of it, and tuning the basic mapping and fuelling parameters via the ECU. The ultimate stage of engine work for your trackday weapon is to fully rebuild the engine in search of greater performance and reliability.

Rebuilding an engine, if it's not something you have experience of, is a job best left to a specialist. The

Fully rebuilt engine, designed for maximum performance. (Author collection)

Shiny new radiator with uprated capacity to maximise cooling ability. (Author collection)

tolerances of the moving parts are amazingly fine, as the rotational speeds are incredibly high and the constituent parts need to maintain perfect alignment. Road car engines are being built with better and better manufacturing tolerances in the hunt for greater economy, performance, and reliability, and you may find, if your car has a modern engine, that there isn't a lot you can do to it to improve its potential. For older engines, however, there are a number of things you should look at.

Reliability is going to be very important. The engine will be running at high revs and under high load for sustained periods, far beyond its intended original use. To avoid potential problems there are three main areas you want to look at: excessive heat build-up, and its dissipation; lubrication, and vibration. The first issue we'll look at is vibration. When an engine is running at high revs, any small difference in the weight of individual components is magnified by their rotational or longitudinal speed. These differences result in vibrations in the engine, which can lead to uneven wear, or even component failure. Balancing the crankshaft, connecting rods, and/ or pistons, reduces these marginal differences which otherwise lead to unwanted vibration. You might have heard the phrase 'to blueprint an engine.' This is the process of taking the balancing to the next level, by re-machining the components to reduce weight and to perfectly match their balance.

As well as improving reliability, balancing also indirectly allows the engine to produce more power and torque, as it runs more efficiently and at higher revs without the damage which might otherwise occur. Balancing the components is a very delicate art: making sure the components in question exactly match each other, whilst removing as little material as possible to avoid weakening them. This is a potentially expensive and time-consuming process, but the results are more than worthwhile.

After balancing the engine, make sure that it's operating at the correct temperature, and isn't running too hot. As you'll spend a lot of time at full throttle and high engine speed, cooling will be of paramount importance. If the water and oil get too hot, the engine can become damaged. If the water temperature is too high, the block will be insufficiently cooled. This will cause the oil to overheat, reducing its viscosity, which means more friction and, therefore, wear.

Check the effectiveness of the water radiator by letting the car reach operating temperature, and then feeling for cool spots in the radiator matrix. Such spots will indicate blockages in the radiator. A few years ago I would have recommended re-coring the radiator, but these days it costs much the same to get a complete replacement unit instead.

If water temperature issues continue, you may need to increase the size of the radiator, or run additional, smaller, units to increase the cooling capacity. Also, it can be worth looking at how the air is ducted to and from the radiator. In most cases, it will be difficult to do much about the air coming in to the radiator, seeing as it usually sits very close to the front of the car, leaving few options for routing air. Once the air has passed through the radiator, however, all that hot air needs to escape the engine bay, otherwise the underbonnet temperature and air pressure can increase, slowing and potentially hampering the passage of cool air through the radiator. The most efficient way of expelling this air is to duct it to vents in the bonnet. These ducts can be shaped to accelerate the air passing out from under the bonnet, reducing the back-pressure. If you can't fit ducts, then vents in the bonnet alone will also help, or you could raise the rear of the bonnet a couple of centimetres or so to give the air an escape route.

You may find that the oil is also running too hot at sustained high revs. If this is the case, you could try fitting an oil cooler (fed via hoses from a bracket fitted to the oil filter housing). An oil cooler is an additional small radiator mounted in the airflow at the front of the

Baffles in a sump. (Courtesy Jamie Packham)

car, cooling the oil in the same way that a conventional water radiator works. This cooled oil is then returned to the filter before being pumped back around the engine. The cooler oil will be running at a viscosity required by the engine at the higher revs.

Once you have the oil at the right

Baffles to keep the oil in the right place and a modified oil pump pickup to avoid engine oil starvation. (Courtesy Jamie Packham)

temperature, you need to make sure it's always flowing around the engine. Your modified track car is lighter, has better brakes, better suspension and stickier tyres than when it left the production line. This means it can stop quicker and corner harder and faster than was originally intended. The upshot of this is that the oil in the sump will be flung around all over the place when, ideally, you need it sitting in the bottom of the sump so the oil pickup can effectively scavenge the oil it needs to keep the engine lubricated. Even having the oil pickup out of the oil for a second can lead to irreparable damage to the bearings in the engine, so it's vital that you keep the oil under control. The lubrication system can be improved by the use of 'baffles' in the sump, or by converting the whole system from a 'wet sump' to a 'dry sump' system.

Baffles are walls, barriers and one-way trap doors built into the base of the sump to control the movement of oil in the sump. Under high cornering loads, instead of all the oil rushing away from the pickup in the base of the sump, the walls and trapdoors restrict the oil flow, keeping a large enough quantity of oil at the pickup point to avoid starvation.

A dry sump system is an extreme solution, and an expensive one, but it is without doubt the best engineering solution. A traditional wet sump system uses a sump to hold a volume of oil. An oil pump, usually driven from the crankshaft, is used to draw oil from this sump through a pickup pipe, whereupon it is distributed around the engine. A dry sump system does away with a large capacity sump, replacing it with a much thinner unit for catching the oil as it's fed to the bottom of the engine via gravity. This oil drains into an external pipe which carries it, via a pump, to an external reservoir. This reservoir has a second pump mounted below it to draw the oil out again, whereupon it is redistributed to the engine. Because the pumps are usually mounted below the reservoir and sump, the oil is fed to the pumps via gravity, rather than being sucked up as in a wet sump system, and so the external reservoir will always be feeding oil out of its base, so there's never a drop in oil pressure through starvation. The engine can be mounted lower (since there's no need for a large wet sump under the crank), helping to lower the car's centre of gravity. Also, as the crank isn't near the main supply of oil, there's no chance of its high rotational speed 'frothing' the oil. Frothed oil has the same lubrication quality as no oil, and it can also damage pumps which are designed for fluids rather than air. Mounting all of the pumps externally means they are much easier to maintain and replace if need be, and the externally-mounted main reservoir can easily be cooled, allowing for efficient temperature control.

Now we've made the engine reliable, you might as well get as much performance from it as you can (and in

A stripped, lightened, caged and track-prepped road car. (Courtesy Jenny South)

this respect size does matter!). If you can increase the size of the pistons you can increase the amount of fuel and air ingested in each combustion cycle. More fuel and air results in a bigger bang, which gives more power and more torque. If you simultaneously improve the flow of air and fuel coming in by modifying the inlet valves, and also improve the flow of exhaust gases going out by modifying the exhaust valves, you can boost the performance even more.

All this means you can tune the engine for running at high revs. You may find, however, that you've made the engine 'lumpy' and awkward to drive at low speeds, but once on track and up in the rev range it will come into its own. Be careful of chasing extreme power figures, though, and remember that torque is arguably more important, as it determines the driveability of the engine and its ability to accelerate out of a corner. There's no point having 1000bhp if it's produced between 9800rpm and 10,000rpm; better to go for less power but in a wider, more usable power band, and increased torque.

Chapter 7

Using and maintaining an ex-race car

By the time you've developed your car using all of the methods described in this book, you'll probably have spent an awful lot of money. For some that's no problem, as the pleasure of building the project and the sense of satisfaction (relief?) on completing it far outweigh the financial hurdle. For others, drip feeding improvements can only come as more funds become available, making it a long-term project of improvement. There are people, though, who either don't

Old race cars make great ready-to-run trackday cars. (Courtesy David Stallard)

This Mini has made the transition from race to trackday to give the owner hours of fun. (Courtesy Jenny South)

Radical trackday car. (Courtesy Jenny South)

The new trackday car from Caterham, the SP300R. (Courtesy Jenny South)

have the time or patience, and will look to buy a ready-to-run track car.

As I mentioned earlier, many manufacturers are now building trackday specials – be it the 'Nürburgring' Special Editions of the Corsa and Astra hot hatches, or the successful and popular Radical brand with its fleet of mini endurance-styled cars, or even the ever popular Caterham/Westfield brands that can be driven to the circuit, raced around for the day, then driven home. These cars make great off-the-shelf trackday cars, and are also perfect for the kinds of upgrades we've talked about in this book; the only difference being the cars are already very good on track, so the upgrades are higher up the options list, and will yield ever smaller returns as you hunt out the last little bits of performance.

An alternative to buying one of

these purpose-built track cars is to invest in an old racing car. A quick trawl through the classifieds on motorsportads.co.uk or racecarsdirect.com reveals a plethora of race metal (or plastic, fibreglass, or carbon-fibre), ready to be taken on track. Before you dive in, though, there are a few things worth considering.

The first thing to consider is the type of car to go for. A Formula Renault single-seater race car may look like huge fun, and may be relatively cheap, but there are very few places to drive it other than circuit test days. To go on a test day you need to have an ARDS racing licence, and all the safety gear (suit, gloves, boots, etc), and generally test days are more expensive than trackdays; there'll be fewer cars, so you'll be sharing the track hire fee with fewer people. Trackday companies no

longer allow single-seater racing cars on their events, as the speed difference is too great, and, because the cars are very small and light, there's a greater danger of injury in the event of a collision with a larger saloon car. I'm not going to describe club racing saloon cars here, since basically they'll have been through the process described in the previous chapters (ie, taking a normal roadgoing vehicle and turning it into a race car, albeit to a specific set of technical regulations governing wheel size, suspension supplier, spring rates, weight, power, etc). Whilst there's scope for development with these, we've already dealt with it in the previous chapters.

The cars to look for are manufacturer-prepared race cars, primarily from single make series. Cars like the Renault Clio Cup, SEAT

Formula Renault single-seater. Fun but limited in driving options. (Courtesy Pieter van Beesten)

Seat SupaCopa Race Car makes a reliable and fun trackday tool. (Courtesy Paul Cherry)

Battle scars on a race car. (Author collection)

Leon Cupra or SupaCopa models, Porsche GT3 Cup, or Ferrari Challenge cars. Depending on what tickles you, for £20-25k you can pick up a fairly modern Clio Cup car (or even one of the mad V6 mid-engined, rear-wheel drive models from the European series). For about £5k more you can find a Mk2 SEAT SupaCopa race car, virtually as quick as a modern touring car, but with bulletproof engine and a trick DSG paddle operated gearbox. Over £30k, and you can pick up a Porsche 996 GT3 Cup car, whilst £55k can get you an early 997 Cup, and £65+ can get you into a Ferrari 360 Challenge car.

Before you get too excited, though,

a word of warning: the running costs for these cars are significantly greater than their roadgoing counterparts. These cars have been built to compete in a flat out environment, so they'll have high-quality components that have a strict lifecycle. A lot of components, such as suspension, brakes or engine parts, will be motorsport specific, or even custom to those types of cars, so getting hold of replacements is difficult and expensive. Even very similar components, but developed for motorsport rather than road, are, generally speaking, considerably more expensive than the road component. Motorsport is like weddings, ask your local hotel if you can

book a room for a large dinner and they will quote you a price. Let slip it's for a wedding and an extra '0' appears on the bill. A motorsport developed component will cost more, even if it appears to be the same as the road component but painted a different colour ...

Let's assume you have the budget to buy, transport, maintain and run an ex-race car. When you've found a couple in the classifieds it's important to go to view them with the right mindset. The key point to remember is they are 'ex-' race cars, ie, they have been involved in racing and will carry some of the battle scars that go with that. Panels might not be in pristine condition, the paint might

Compressor and wheel gun. (Author collection)

have done (not necessarily how old they are), if you have a car with provenance, ie, a famous livery, or history of good performances, or famous drivers, these will increase the value almost regardless of the condition.

Also, think about the extra tools you will need. You might need to get a compressor with some air bottles and lines for the compressed air jacks on the car, you will then need the specific stands to rest the car on once it's up in the air. Changing a wheel might need air guns or similar, especially if the car has centre-lock wheels rather than a traditional four- or five-stud setup.

Finally, don't forget that you'll need a trailer and a tow vehicle. Even if you went to the trouble of registering the car for the road, it would be so compromised, harsh, recalcitrant, loud and awkward on the road, that the hassle of loading it on the trailer will seem, without doubt, the easy option.

One final aspect to think about is noise. Race cars are built to run at race meetings, where the maximum permitted noise is usually much higher than that of a trackday. Trackdays run at anywhere from 95db through to 105db in the UK, but racing cars are generally louder. Club race meetings in the UK are restricted to 105-108db, whilst National events, such as the BTCC and Formula 3, or visiting series, such as the Boss Formula and DTM, can run up to 118db. When you consider adding 10db is the equivalent of ten times the power produced, just adding 3db roughly doubles the power, reducing the noise levels to an acceptable level for a trackday can be difficult and expensive.

If you're planning on running an ex-race car, think also about your long-term objectives. If you plan to race the car after doing some trackdays, or selling it on to someone else, it's best to try and keep the car as original as possible. This keeps the door open for the car to slot back into its racing series without falling foul of eligibility requirements. If you're viewing it as a long-term project, for you to keep and enjoy, then feel free to tune and develop the car to your heart's content.

not match from one part of the car to another, and closer inspection may well uncover previous accident damage. Racing cars have a hard life and, as the saying goes, 'it ain't the years, it's the mileage,' or rather the abuse they have suffered during that mileage. This also makes them quite hard to price as well, as, whilst the majority of cars will be more expensive the less racing they

A great car but those noisy side-exit exhausts might fall foul of the noise police on a trackday. (Courtesy Paul Cherry)

Chapter 8

Trackday organisers

This chapter is a simple reference containing contact details of the various main trackday companies in operation in the UK at the time of writing. The list is broken down into the types of venues involved: handling events; airfield; club circuit; and Grand Prix circuits. The companies listed in each category usually run events on a number of different types of track, but tend to specialise in the event type under which they're listed. Each contact notes if they're a member of the Association of Trackday Organisers (ATDO), the trackday governing body which ensures standards are met across the industry.

Readers outside the UK should check online for their nearest organisers.

HANDLING EVENTS
Car control and drift days.

Caterham Drift Experience, Caterham Cars Ltd, Station Avenue, Caterham, Surrey, CR3 6LB
Tel: 01883 333700
Email: experience.caterham.co.uk
ATDO: No

Motorsport Events
Tel: 0844 873 6075
www.motorsport-events.co.uk
ATDO: No

Drift What Ya Brung
Santa Pod Raceway, Airfield Road, Podington, Wellingborough, Northamptonshire, NN29 7XA
Tel: 01234 782828
www.dwyb.co.uk
ATDO: No

AIRFIELD TRACKDAYS
Temporary circuits laid out using airfield runways and perimeter roads.

Motorsport Events
Tel: 0844 873 6075
www.motorsport-events.co.uk
ATDO: No

Javelin Trackdays
Mulberry Close, Keelby, Immingham, Lincolnshire, DN41 8EX
Tel: 01469 560574
www.javelintrackdays.co.uk
ATDO: Yes

CLUB CIRCUIT TRACKDAYS
Circuits used by club racers across the country such as Cadwell Park, Snetterton, Castle Combe and Donington.

Anglesey Circuit
Ty Croes, Anglesey, LL63 5TF
Tel: 01407 811400
www.angleseycircuit.com
ATDO: Yes

Apex Trackdays Ltd
Ardeevin, Crossings Road, Chapel en le Frith, Derbyshire, SK23 9RX
Tel: 08448 581 591
www.apextrackdays.co.uk
ATDO: Yes

BHP Trackdays Ltd
23 Rushfords, Lingfield, Surrey, RH7 6EG
Tel: 01342 837957
www.trackdays.co.uk
ATDO: Yes

Castle Combe Circuit
Castle Combe, Chippenham, Wiltshire, SN14 7EY
Tel: 01249 782417
www.castlecombecircuit.co.uk
ATDO: No

Circuit Days Ltd
Roydene, Bawtry Road, Tickhill, Doncaster, South Yorkshire, DN11 9HA
Tel: 01302 743827

Airfield trackday. (Courtesy Steve Clarke)

Club circuit trackday taking place on the famous Goodwood circuit. (Courtesy Jenny South)

A Golf R32 thundering down Paddock Hill Bend at Brands Hatch. (Courtesy Jenny South)

An MX5 at Goodwood. (Courtesy Jenny South)

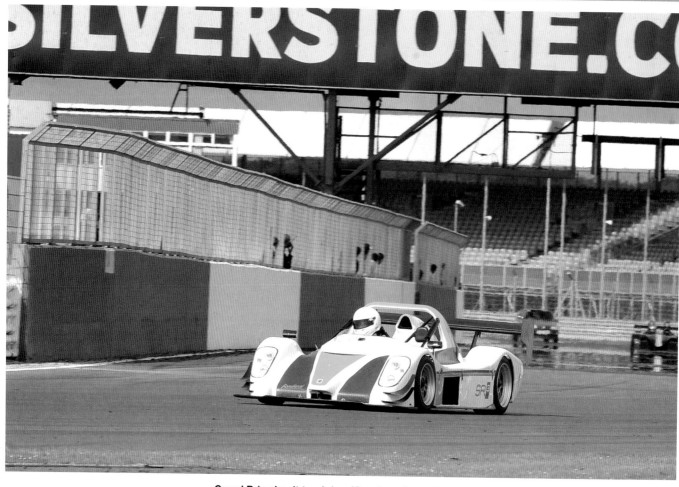

Grand Prix circuit trackday. (Courtesy Jenny South)

www.circuit-days.co.uk
ATDO: Yes

Club MSV (MotorSport Vision)
Alex Baker / MSV Brands Hatch Circuit,
Fawkham, Longfield, Kent, DA3 8NG
Tel: 0870 850 5014
www.clubmsv.co.uk
ATDO: Yes

Donington Park
Donington Park, Castle Donington,
Leicestershire, DE74 2RP
Tel: 01332 810048
www.donington-park.co.uk
ATDO: Yes

Javelin Trackdays
Mulberry Close, Keelby, Immingham,
Lincolnshire, DN41 8EX
Tel: 01469 560574

www.javelintrackdays.co.uk
ATDO: Yes

Knockhill Race Circuit
Dunfermline, Fife, KY12 9TF
Tel: 01383 723337
www.knockhill.co.uk
ATDO: Yes

Lotus On Track
Lotus on Track Ltd, PO Box 1217,
Maidstone, Kent, ME14 9JR
www.lotus-on-track.com
ATDO: No

Opentrack Events Ltd
45 Jeavons Lane, Great Cambourne,
Cambridge, Cambridgeshire, CB23 6AF
Tel: 01954 202588
www.opentrack.co.uk
ATDO: Yes

Rockingham Motor Speedway
Mitchell Road, Corby, Northamptonshire,
NN17 8TQ
Tel: 01536 271534
www.rockingham.co.uk
ATDO: Yes

Silverstone Circuits Ltd
Silverstone Circuit, Silverstone,
Northamptonshire, NN12 8TN
Tel: 01327 320406
www.silverstone.co.uk
ATDO: Yes

Trackskills
15 Belfast Road, Nutts Corner, Crumlin,
Co Antrim, BT29 4TQ
Tel: 028 9082 5235
www.trackskills.com
ATDO: Yes

A variety of cars on the Brooklands/Luffield complex at Silverstone. (Courtesy Jenny South)

GRAND PRIX CIRCUIT TRACKDAYS

Organisers who use the large GP venues here and abroad, such as Silverstone, Spa, Barcelona, and the Nürburgring.

BookaTrack.com Ltd
50 Deykin Road, Lichfield, Staffordshire, WS13 6PS
Tel: 0843 2084635
www.bookatrack.com
ATDO: Yes

Gold Track
Little Preston House, Little Preston, Northamptonshire, NN11 3TF
Tel: 01327 361361
www.goldtrack.co.uk
ATDO: Yes

Ringweekends Ltd
12 Green Lane North, Coventry, West Midlands, CV3 6DF
Tel: 07768 058550
www.destination-Nürburgring.com
ATDO: Yes

RMA Ltd
PO Box 1810, Maidenhead, Berkshire, SL6 1YX
Tel: 0845 260 4545
www.rmatrackdays.com
ATDO: Yes

Wheelsports Ltd
188 Empress Road, Southampton, Hampshire, SO14 0JY
Tel: 02380 330668
www.wheelsports.co.uk
ATDO: Yes

Chapter 9

Insurance

Most insurance companies have cottoned on to the trackday market, and the potential for losses or claims therein, and have specific exclusions for trackday driving (and a lot even explicitly preclude cover for the Nürburgring).

Motorsport insurance companies have also seen the expansion in the trackday market, and have leapt in to offer cover for your pride and joy on a trackday. But the big question is: is it worth it?

Well, ultimately, that's a question only you can answer, so I'll give you some of the facts and you can make up your own mind.

First, virtually no insurance company will cover mechanical damage, ie, an engine or gearbox failure, but will cover fire and accident damage. One thing with trackdays, though, is they are generally very safe. Compared to a race event, for example, the driving on track is generally courteous and respectful, so the chance of car-to-car contact is extremely slim. In fact, I'd be surprised if, statistically, it wasn't less likely than on the drive to the circuit. Your biggest chance of damage is going off when

your enthusiasm gets the better of the available grip. Depending on which circuit you're on, weather conditions, and where you lose it, a slip-up can result in anything from a harmless spin to contact with something immovable. Take Silverstone, for example; as it's built to modern F1 standards, the circuit is ringed with vast expanses of tarmac runoff. This gives you plenty of opportunity to rescue an 'off,' or simply spin harmlessly to a halt. However, Club Corner and Woodcote Corner are both favourites for driver error, and if the car spins to the inside on either of those, you're more than likely going to hit the pit walls, especially when you bear in mind that anything solid on a circuit tends to act as a magnet for out-of-control cars.

Insurance, then, is good for peace of mind, but, apart from the cost of the insurance itself, bear in mind the overall outlay in the event of an accident. Let's say, for example, you insure your car for a trackday for a premium of £250. Unfortunately, on the day you have a little spin which results in a small knock on the barrier and some damage. No problem; you have insurance. Once you claim, though, you'll still have to pay

the excess, let's say £2000. So, already your accident has to cause more than £2250 of damage before it becomes worthwhile having the insurance. Consider as well that you'll probably be doing a number of trackdays that year, let's say six, for argument's sake, and you have this accident on the last day. You've already forked out £1500 worth of premiums, in addition to your £2000 excess, and suddenly you need to have a REALLY big shunt to make it worthwhile. It's also worth bearing in mind that, with some insurance companies, the percentage of any payout that can be paid to labour costs can be limited, so you might still be out of pocket at the end of the day.

Now, I'm not saying 'don't get insurance,' but have a good think about it and bear in mind the actual value of the insurance relative to the value of the item being insured. If the car you use on track is your everyday runabout, then it might be more important to have some form of cover in place to minimise any downtime you have without the car. If the car is an expensive super or hyper car, it'll probably be worth it for the peace of mind (plus you can probably afford it without even noticing). If you

Could this 'off' result in an insurance claim? (Courtesy Paul Cherry)

have a lower cost track car, it might not be worth it. You can probably fix minor damage yourself, and anything major might just mean the car becomes disposable. Plan it out carefully, and do plenty of research, as the premiums can vary massively, from £70 a day if multiple events are booked, through to £1000+ for an exotic car with multiple drivers on a one-off event.

Damage repairs can be claimed from an insurer, but read the small print. (Courtesy Paul Cherry)

Chapter 10
Going racing

So, what do you need to do if you want to go on to the next level and enter a motor race? Going racing is very easy for trackday drivers, possibly more so now than it's ever been. Depending on the car you drive, and the budget you can set aside for racing, there's a wide range of options for you to choose from. MSVR, the racing club arm of the MSV group of circuits, has recently launched its Trackday Trophy series (www.trackdaytrophy.co.uk), designed so trackday drivers can experience motor racing with the minimum of fuss. The series caters for saloon-type cars, and has fairly open regulations, so the car you've been developing as a trackday car can be used as the race

Going racing. (Courtesy David Stallard)

A variety of vehicles make good race cars. (Courtesy David Stallard)

car with little or no modification needed (depending on the prior development). In fact, as long as the car has a roll cage, electrical cutoff switch, four-point harness or above, and a fire extinguisher, it's ready to race. Along similar lines, the Classic Sports Car Club (www. classicsportscarclub.co.uk) runs a number of different series now, which cater for almost every car imaginable, and promote value for money track time and a real 'grass roots' spirit; so you don't have to have the latest and greatest bit of kit to be competitive and enjoy your weekend of racing. All of the series mentioned comprise around 40min races with mandatory pitstops to allow for driver changes, so you have the chance to go racing with a buddy and share the costs.

The one thing you will need to do before you sign up to your first race meeting is to get yourself a licence. This is not simply a case of posting an application form; you need to pass written and practical tests.

GETTING A LICENCE
In the UK, the first thing to do to start the licence application ball rolling is to contact the Motor Sports Association. The MSA will send you your 'Go Racing' starter pack. This contains: your Licence Application Form; *Go Racing* video detailing the application process,

testing procedure and basics of starting racing; *MSA Yearbook* which details all the rules and regulations of motorsport in the UK plus a useful directory; a *Starting Motorsport* handbook full of hints and tips, and; an Association of Racing Drivers School (ARDS) leaflet, with contact information for the ARDS registered schools.

The MSA can be contacted at:
MSA Motorsports House
Riverside Park
Colnbrook
Slough
SL3 0HG
Telephone: 01753 765000
Web: www.msauk.org

Once you've got your pack, read the booklets, and studied the rules included in the *Yearbook* (also known as the *Blue Book*), contact one of the ARDS registered schools to organise a date for your ARDS test (contact details below). This will be comprised of a multiple choice written test on the basic rules and regulations of motorsport, and a practical test on the circuit with an ARDS registered instructor who will assess your practical ability. You must pass both tests to be granted a licence. The written test asks such questions as the meaning of different flag signals, whereas the practical test is all about competence.

Your practical test will last an unspecified number of laps, and, after being shown the circuit by your instructor, you'll be required to complete laps, with little or no instruction; consistently, accurately, and with awareness of other track users. Speed is fairly irrelevant, as long as you're circulating relatively briskly. The instructor isn't looking for outright pace, but rather that you're aware of and courteous to other track users, and that you can consistently take the correct line in the corners.

Passing the test will grant you a Race National 'B' licence. The licence system in motorsport is graded, and this is the first one you will acquire. The National 'B' entitles you to race in most championships and cars in the UK.

To upgrade your licence, you'll need to gain signatures from the Clerks of the Course for any races you've completed. When you sign on in the morning, you'll be given the option of surrendering your licence to the Clerk for the day, who will, if you successfully complete your race, sign and return it at the end of the day.

To upgrade to a National 'A' licence, you'll need to obtain six signatures on your licence from completed races, and resubmit your licence to the MSA, along with the extra fee for the higher grade licence. One signature can also be obtained by marshalling at a race event. A National 'A' licence will entitle you

Develop your track car into a race car. (Courtesy David Stallard)

Historic racer using a trackday for some extra testing. (Courtesy Jenny South)

to race more powerful and high profile cars in the UK, such as Touring Cars or Formula 3, as well as race in Europe if your UK based championship or series visits those countries.

To upgrade to an International 'C' licence, you'll need to obtain three signatures from completed National 'A' races, and for an International Historic licence, you'll need to obtain five signatures on a National 'B' licence.

ARDS REGISTERED SCHOOLS

You'll only be able to take your racing licence test at an ARDS (Association of Racing Driver School) registered school. At the time of writing these are as follows:

Thruxton Motorsport Centre
Thruxton Circuit
Andover
Hampshire
SP11 8PW
01264 882222
www.thruxtonracing.co.uk

Aintree Racing Drivers School Ltd
Three Sisters Race Circuit
Bryn Road
Ashton-in-Makerfield
Wigan, Lancashire
WN4 8DD
01942 270230
www.racing-school.co.uk

Anglesey Circuit
Estate Office
Bodorgan
Anglesey
North Wales
LL62 5LP
01407 840253

www.angleseycircuit.com

Castle Combe Racing School
Castle Combe Circuit
Chippenham
Wiltshire
SN14 7EY
01249 782929
www.castlecomberacingschool.co.uk

Croft Circuit
Croft-on-Tees
North Yorkshire
DL2 2PN
01325 721819
www.croftcircuit.co.uk

Everyman Motor Racing
Mallory Park Circuit
Leicestershire
01455 841670
www.everymanracing.co.uk

Knockhill Racing Circuit
Dunfermline
Fife
Scotland
01383 723337
www.knockhill.co.uk

Silverstone Motorsport Academy
Silverstone
Northamptonshire
NN12 8TJ
01327 857413
www.silverstone-circuit.co.uk

Readers outside the UK should check online for their nearest school.

PERSONAL EQUIPMENT

Trackdays normally only require that you wear a helmet as special equipment.

Racing, however, is a different matter. When racing, the likelihood of an accident is much greater, so it's important to be properly protected.

The best places to shop for your gear are the specialist shops, such as Road and Race Gear, Grand Prix Racewear, and Demon Tweeks. If you can make a personal visit rather than shopping via the internet, you'll find the staff able to help and advise on the best kit for your budget.

The helmet is probably of the foremost importance, as this protects your head. Don't skimp on the helmet, but get the best lid you can afford. It's also worth looking into getting a HANS Device. This is a collar, worn under the seatbelts, which attaches to the helmet and limits head movement, and hence neck injuries, in the case of an accident. Some series require the HANS Device as a mandatory piece of driver's equipment, so it's worth checking the regulations for the series you want to enter.

You should also look to get a high quality race suit, preferably with two or three layers of fireproof protection. When you get to the gloves and boots, make sure they are comfortable above all else, and give you a good sense of touch and feel, as these are your primary points of contact with the car.

Once you have all the essentials, look at purchasing additional safety gear, such as fire-proof underwear, as it's always best to be prepared for the worst. If you plan on racing in Europe, some of these items are mandatory, and you should consult the local regulations and the MSA General Regulations for Competitors (Blue Book) for advice.

Essential driver's kit. (Courtesy Pieter van Beesten)

Chapter 11
Keep it on the black stuff!

I hope the book has been informative, and has given you an idea of the direction to go in when buying, tuning and developing your trackday car.

Trackdays can be immense fun, and, by tuning and developing your chosen ride between events, you get the satisfaction and pleasure of creating the car you want to drive, and then going and fulfilling its promise on some of the most famous bits of tarmac in the world.

Have fun, stay safe, and keep it on the black stuff!

Have fun! (Courtesy Pieter van Beesten)

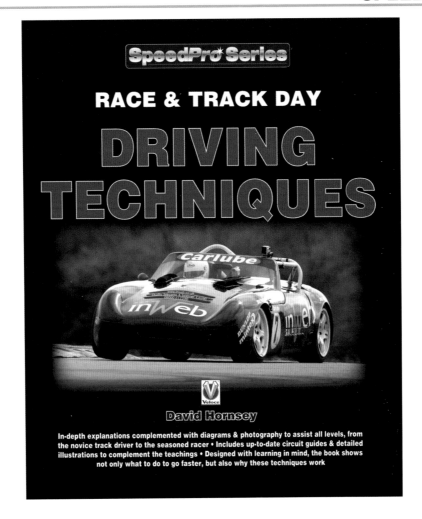

SpeedPro Series

RACE & TRACK DAY
DRIVING TECHNIQUES

David Hornsey

In-depth explanations complemented with diagrams & photography to assist all levels, from the novice track driver to the seasoned racer • Includes up-to-date circuit guides & detailed illustrations to complement the teachings • Designed with learning in mind, the book shows not only what to do to go faster, but also why these techniques work

ISBN: 978-1-845843-55-7
Paperback • 25x20.7cm • £14.99* UK/$29.95* USA
• 128 pages • 100 pictures

For more info on Veloce titles, visit our website at
www.veloce.co.uk • email: info@veloce.co.uk • Tel:
+44(0)1305 260068
* prices subject to change, p&p extra

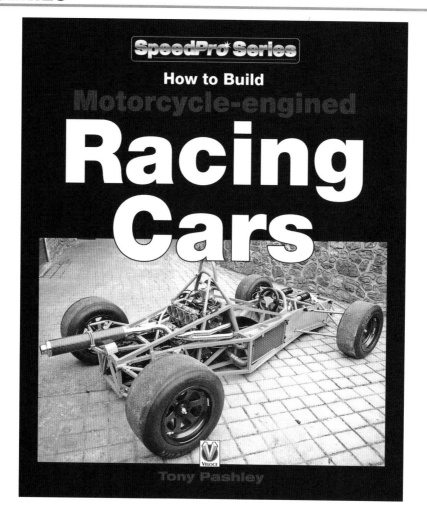

ISBN: 978-1-845841-23-2
Paperback • 25x20.7cm
• £24.99* UK/$49.95* USA
• 128 pages • 416 colour and b&w pictures

For more info on Veloce titles, visit our website at
www.veloce.co.uk • email: info@veloce.co.uk
• Tel: +44(0)1305 260068
* prices subject to change, p&p extra

Ebook only

ISBN: 978-1-845845-06-3
Prices vary depending on retailer
152 colour and b&w pictures

For more info on Veloce titles, visit our website at
www.veloce.co.uk • email: info@veloce.co.uk
• Tel: +44(0)1305 260068

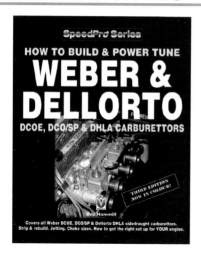

**ISBN: 978-1-903706-75-6
Paperback • 25x20.7cm •
£19.99* UK/$39.95* USA •
128 pages • 181 colour and
b&w pictures**

**ISBN: 978-1-84584-162-1
Paperback • 25x20.7cm
• £19.99* UK/$39.95* USA
• 128 pages • 164 colour and
b&w pictures**

**ISBN: 978-1-84584-207-9
Paperback • 25x20.7cm
• £19.99* UK/$39.95* USA
• 128 pages • 118 photos and
illustrations**

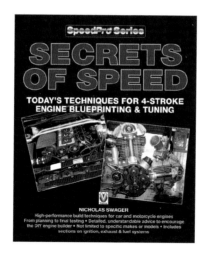

**ISBN: 978-1-845842-97-0
Paperback • 25x20.7cm
• £9.99* UK/$19.95* USA
• 128 pages • 201 colour and
b&w pictures**

   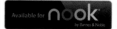  

Index

NOTES